The Reason for Everything

ROBERT GOUGE

Copyright 2025 Robert Gouge

All rights reserved.

ISBN: 979-8-218-61829-2

DEDICATION

To Steven, Jonathan, and Nickolas without whom this work would not have been possible.

Table of Contents

PREFACE 1
    The Allegory of the Cave 2
    The Matrix 4
The Will to Power 7
    My Definition 7
    History & Origin 10
    Keep Going! 15
The Will to Power in Nature 16
    Evolution 16
    A Single Cell 16
    Charles Darwin's Finches 17
    Predator and Prey 18
    Homo Habilis to Modern Humans 19
    Visualizing the Will to Power 23
    A Cosmic Force 24
    Conclusion 25
The Will to Power in Technology 26
    Cellular Phones and Smartphones 26
    Video Games 30
    How it Started versus How it's Going 34
The Will to Power in Humans 39
    "Good" and "Bad" do not Apply 39
    Habits: Reflections of the Will to Power 40
    8 Billion Minds and Counting 41
    If it can be Cheated, it will be Cheated 43
    Thoughts are Things 45

Relationships: Humans with Humans 46

Conclusion 67

How to use the Will to Power 70

Change & Habit Formation 70

A Few Thoughts on Free Will 75

Analysis & Prediction 75

Implications of the Will to Power 80

The Future of Humanity 80

A Future with Artificial Intelligence 81

A Positive Return to Humanity 86

Reflections of the Will to Power 88

The Will to Power: The Undeniable Constant 88

The Journey You've Taken 88

A Final Example: The Will to Power in Action 89

The Reason for Everything as a Case Study of The Will to Power 90

Final Proof: The Universal Law of Refinement 94

The Core of The Framework: 95

The Will to Power in Entropy 96

The Will to Power in Light Speed 100

The Will to Power in Absolute Zero 103

The Will to Power in Intelligence and Computation 106

The Will to Power in Quantum Superposition 109

The Will to Power in Brownian Motion 112

The Will to Power in Evolution (Biological and Technological) 114

The Will to Power in Chemical Equilibrium and Reaction Limits 117

The Will to Power in Information Theory and Signal Processing 119

Final Words 121

PREFACE

Within the pages of this book, you will learn about the singular driving force of all things—the reason for everything.

Understanding this force and how it moves through everything in existence has the potential to *greatly* alter the way you view your life, your world, and the very nature of existence itself. It is for this reason that I am compelled to write this preface and offer a few words of caution.

Once you learn the idea presented in this book and begin to see the true driving force of all things, it cannot be unseen, it cannot be unlearned, and it cannot be forgotten. No two minds on this earth are identical, so one cannot say how learning the ideas I intend to explain may affect you and the way you view the world. It can easily lead to a state of enlightenment and calm, or it can, just as easily, drive one to nihilism and apathy.

For me, learning about the one force behind all things caused me to become disillusioned with areas of my life that were once rooted in mystery, intrigue, and magic.

For example, romantic love and the pursuit of that love used to be *the* driving force of my life. I was a hopeless romantic at heart and firmly believed in the ideas behind romantic love, such as the notion that there is someone out there for everyone. I believed that a 'soulmate' existed—someone who completed me as I completed them, a perfect union of two becoming one.

However, once I became enlightened and started to perceive the one driving force moving through all things, the mystery and magic that fueled my romantic desires were replaced with understanding and logic. Gone were the butterflies in my stomach, gone were the heart flutters, and gone was my willingness to sacrifice everything in the name of romantic love—a drive that once fueled and moved me so completely.

I could now see why my past romantic relationships had failed and why some relationships around me succeeded. In my mind, the mystery was solved, and the magic was gone.

Learning about the one force behind all things disenchanted romantic love for me, and because this knowledge cannot be unlearned, I know that I will never get it back. Yet, what I gained far outweighs what I lost. With understanding and logic came clarity and peace, replacing anxiety and confusion with calm and insight. To see the force that moves through all things is to unlock a hidden layer of existence, one that allows you to navigate life and its challenges with unparalleled insight.

The Allegory of the Cave

This word of caution regarding enlightenment has been issued many times before, by many people. A prime example of such a warning is the Greek philosopher Plato's *Allegory of the Cave* from his work *Republic*, which I will attempt to summarize here.

In this allegory, Socrates gives an example of people who have lived within a cave since birth. They are chained in such a way that their heads and bodies are fixed. They cannot look around at the cave, themselves, or the others chained alongside them. They can only stare at the fire-illuminated cave wall in front of them. They are prisoners.

Upon this wall, shadows are cast, as people place objects in front of a fire burning behind the chained prisoners. Someone holds a shovel in front of the fire, and its shadow is cast upon the cave wall. They tell the captives, "This is a shovel." The captives know not of the burning fire behind them, the people holding the objects and making the sounds, or that the images they see upon the wall are merely shadows. To each of them, their reality is that the silhouettes and sounds upon the wall are 'real,' despite these things not being an accurate representation of the world.

An Illustration of The Allegory of the Cave, from Plato's Republic. © Jim Tierney, available under a Creative Commons Attribution-ShareAlike 3.0 Unported license. Image source: Wikimedia Commons

Socrates goes on to suggest that these prisoners would not desire to leave the cave because they know no better life. If a prisoner were enlightened—freed and allowed to look around the cave, at the fire, and at the people creating the shadows—it would only make him wish to return to the wall and what is familiar. The shadows upon the wall are clearer to him than the rest of the fire-illuminated cave; the light is too bright for his eyes. When told that what he is seeing now is real—the fire, the people, the world that exists within the rest of the cave—and not the shadows cast upon the wall, the prisoner would not believe it.

Over time, the prisoner's eyes would adjust to the brightness of the fire and the expanse of the cave. He would see the fire and how the shadows were cast upon the cave wall. He would begin to understand that what he thought was reality was something else entirely. The prisoner would reach a new stage of understanding and enlightenment about the world around him.

Socrates then dials this idea up a notch. What if you were to forcibly drag a prisoner out of the cave and into the sunlight—into the real world with sun and grass and stars and trees?

Socrates continues by suggesting that the prisoner would be angry and in pain as he was dragged up and out of the cave. The sun's light would become brighter and brighter until the prisoner is finally left lying blind upon the grass underneath the world-illuminating glow of the sun.

Again, over time, the prisoner's eyes would slowly begin to adjust as they did with the fire in the cave. At first, he would only be able to make out shapes and shadows amidst the blinding light. Then, he would begin to see the moon and the stars of the night. Finally, once his eyes had completely adjusted, he would see the green of the grass, the blue of the sky, and would even gaze upon the sun itself. The prisoner was now further enlightened and saw the world as it truly was. He was free.

The prisoner would believe that this new life was superior to that of life in the cave and he would pity the fellow prisoners he left behind. He would want to share this new reality with the other prisoners and venture back into the cave. However, because his eyes were now accustomed to the light, the darkness of the cave was blinding.

The man would fumble through the darkness, unable to see, until he would reach the other prisoners. He would explain to them the journey he had taken and that he could no longer see within the darkness of the cave. The remaining prisoners would infer that the man's journey had blinded and harmed him and that they should not take a similar journey.

Socrates concluded that if the prisoners who remained in the cave were able, they would kill anyone who attempted to make them take a similar journey—despite hearing the story of the man who returned and the new life he described. The prisoners would fight against their own enlightenment.

Quite the allegory, wouldn't you say? How would you convince the prisoners that what they know as reality isn't real? How do you explain to someone that everything they know is a lie, or at best, a complete distortion of what is real? This leads to a more modern example: *The Matrix*

The Matrix

A modern example of the *Allegory of the Cave* appears in the 1999 film *The Matrix*. In this movie, the protagonist, Neo, is born into a computer-simulated world. The simulated world exactly resembles the world as it was during the late 1990s.

Neo is born, grows up, goes to school, goes on dates, and makes friends, all of whom are also trapped inside this simulated reality—similar to the prisoners of the cave in the prior example. Neo goes to work, gets lunch at his favorite noodle shop, and goes about his life.

However, he starts feeling as though something isn't right with the world. He becomes uneasy about his existence, with no explanation to be found—until he is offered a choice.

Neo is discovered and introduced to a man called Morpheus. The two sit and talk. Morpheus tries to explain to Neo that his world is not the world as it truly is—it is not the real world. He tells Neo that he is a slave, born into bondage, born into a prison he cannot smell, taste, or touch—a prison for his mind.

As you would expect, Morpheus is unable to convince Neo of the truth using words alone. Just like the prisoners in the cave, Neo didn't believe what Morpheus was telling him. Morpheus is, of course, not surprised by this reaction and states, "Unfortunately, no one can be told what the Matrix is. You have to see it for yourself." He offers Neo the choice.

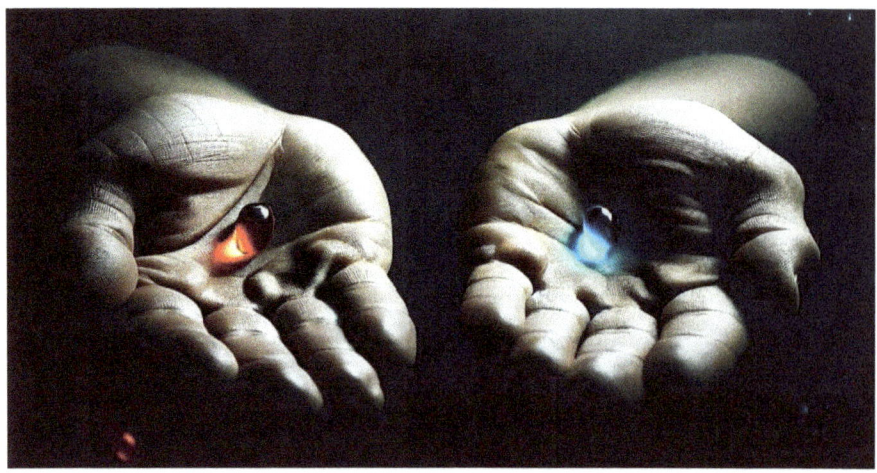

© 2025 Robert Gouge. Exclusive use for The Reason for Everything. All rights reserved.

Morpheus holds out his hands. In one hand, he holds a red pill, and in the other, a blue pill. He tells Neo, "Take the blue pill, and you can wake up at home, in your bed, and believe whatever you want to believe. Take the red pill... and I will show you how deep the rabbit hole goes."

Of course, Neo chooses the red pill, and the following scenes in the movie depict him forcibly removed from the computer-simulated world and into the dystopian wasteland that is reality. This mirrors how the prisoner in Plato's allegory was forcibly dragged into the sunlight. Neo was now free.

The point of this preface and the two examples I've shared is simple: Once you leave the cave or the computer-simulated dream world and become enlightened, you cannot go back.

It should be noted, however, that in all the examples I've shared about enlightenment, including my own, the person attaining the new understanding of their world would never choose to go back to ignorance and darkness. While some things may be lost through the journey, countless others are gained.

So, there it is—I've said my piece. This cautionary preface may seem a bit hyperbolic, but my conscience will rest easy knowing that I have given you what's most important: the right to choose.

Should you continue, I encourage you to take your time with this reading and thoroughly digest each idea as it is presented. The path to enlightenment can be daunting, but it can also yield many gifts. My hope is that as you read on, you'll find not only answers but also inspiration.

Now, if you're ready to see reality broken down to a singular, driving force that explains everything, then I suppose I should start by telling you its name.

It's called...

The Will to Power

Before you can understand the Will to Power, we must first establish a foundation from which everything else will be built. This chapter will serve as that foundation.

I will begin by breaking down and explaining the concept of the Will to Power. Since it can be challenging to grasp, I'll start by sharing my definition and analysis. To further solidify my interpretation, I'll delve into the term's origins and historical context. I'll also highlight examples of how others have referenced the Will to Power in their works, even if they referred to it by a different name.

While the definitions and history may feel abstract at first, the examples I provide later in this book will greatly clarify the concept, helping you fully grasp the Will to Power—what it is, how it works, and why it is the reason for everything.

If you're unfamiliar with philosophical ideas, this section may seem challenging, but I assure you, the effort will be worth it. The deeper you go, the clearer it becomes.

Let's begin our journey of understanding.

My Definition

In order to begin our journey of understanding, we'll need a starting point. We'll start with the most obvious question: "What is the Will to Power?"

Here is my definition of the Will to Power as I've come to understand it:

> *"The Will to Power is the absolute and supreme force that moves through all things that exist or have yet to exist. It is an unbiased, unwavering, unstoppable force that races towards the Asymptrex in a never-*

> *ending cycle of culling, optimization, and refinement that leads all things to their eventuality: to their perfect state or to their demise."*

Obviously not the most concise or easily understood definition, but I believe it to be accurate in defining what the Will to Power is. Let's break this definition down further and make it a bit easier to understand.

"The Will to Power is the supreme and absolute force that moves through all things that exist or have yet to exist."

The one constant of the Will to Power is that it moves, always. That is what it does. Not only does it move through all things in existence such as people, plants, animals, and even inanimate objects, but it also moves through the Unseen as evident by things coming into existence that did not exist before—like thoughts or ideas. For example, the very idea of the Will to Power itself was hidden away in the Unseen before manifesting as a thought in the minds of past thinkers.

It should also be noted that I said, "all things" within my definition above. Without exception, there is *nothing* that the Will to Power does not move through directly or indirectly. There is not one thing in existence that cannot be analyzed to a point at which you can see the Will to Power's influence. It is the one true constant of the universe.

"It is an unbiased, unwavering, unstoppable force that races towards the Asymptrex in a never-ending cycle of culling, optimization, and refinement that leads all things to their eventuality: to their perfect state or to their demise."

In saying that the Will to Power is "unbiased," I am referring to the fact that it is beyond all concepts of good and evil or right and wrong. These concepts simply do not apply. The Will to Power simply races toward eventuality. It does not try to move toward "right" or "happy" outcomes and avoid "wrong" or "bad" outcomes.

It will move through a lifelong drug addict who eventually dies by overdose just as easily and thoroughly as it will move through a medical student who eventually goes on to cure cancer and transform modern medicine. In both cases, the Will to Power behaves in the only way it can behave; by moving, culling, improving, and refining the individuals such that they race toward their Asymptrex or eventual conclusion, whatever that may be.

I use the term "Asymptrex" to describe the point of absolution that the Will to Power is always racing toward. It is the point of conclusion for whatever the Will to Power is moving through—the state of absolute perfection that the Will to Power wants to achieve.

However, I have come to believe that it is impossible for the Will to Power to ever reach the Asymptrex. Upon reaching the Asymptrex, the Will to Power will have reached "perfection," meaning there is no further refinement needed as its form is perfect and can no longer be improved upon. It would be a state of complete dominance without opposition, or complete submission free of dominant influence, or complete balance and equilibrium. Such a state of perfection would cause the Will to Power to cease existing. As such, in the same way that the Will to Power exists and moves through everything, "perfection" is always just out of reach and impossible to attain; they are, in essence, one. The image below is a graphical representation of the Will to Power racing toward the Asymptrex. The Will to Power is signified by the strands of light and energy, while the Asymptrex is depicted as the blinding light in the center.

*The Will to Power racing toward the Asymptrex. Image generated using OpenAI's DALL·E technology. ©
2024 OpenAI.*

History & Origin

With a clear definition established, we can deepen our understanding of this concept by exploring the historical and philosophical origins of the Will to Power.

Friedrich Nietzsche

When examining the emergence of the Will to Power as a topic of philosophical analysis and debate, we need look no further than Friedrich Nietzsche.

Friedrich Nietzsche portrait, public domain image.

Born in 1844, Nietzsche was a prolific German philosopher credited with coining the term "Will to Power," which prominently appeared in his seminal work *Thus Spoke Zarathustra*. In this text, Nietzsche writes:

> *"Where I found a living creature, there I found will to power; and even in the will of the servant I found the will to be master."*[1]

---

[1] Friedrich Nietzsche, *Thus Spoke Zarathustra: A Book for All and None*, trans. Walter Kaufmann (New York: Modern Library, 1995), Part II, "Of Self-Overcoming."

While the idea of a driving force behind existence was not entirely new—having been touched upon by philosophers like Arthur Schopenhauer and Immanuel Kant—Nietzsche is regarded as the first to thoroughly analyze and expand the concept. Drawing inspiration from Schopenhauer's *The World as Will and Representation*, Nietzsche redefined the "Will" from a mere drive for survival to an amoral, universal force he called the Will to Power. He identified it as the essence of all beings, a dynamic force striving for expression, self-overcoming, and mastery—particularly in humans.

Where my interpretation identifies the Asymptrex as the culmination of the Will to Power's manifestation, Nietzsche rejected the notion of any final endpoint. For him, the Will to Power thrived in its eternal movement, existing in a perpetual state of eternal recurrence. It drives creation and transformation not toward any culmination, but through a continuous process of self-overcoming. In Nietzsche's view, each achieved state becomes a steppingstone for further striving, fueling an endless cycle of creation, growth, mastery, and destruction—as seen here in a quote from his work *Beyond Good and Evil*:

> *"The world itself eternally creates itself, eternally destroys itself, in an eternal self-equal rhythm of coming-to-be and passing away."*[2]

One might argue that Nietzsche's concept of the Übermensch (Overman) suggests that he did see an endpoint in relation to his views on the Will to Power. The Übermensch represents the ideal individual who transcends human limitations by rejecting conventional morality and societal norms—harnessing their own will to create new values, embrace life as it is, and shape their reality with authenticity, creativity, and strength.

---

[2] Friedrich Nietzsche, *Beyond Good and Evil: Prelude to a Philosophy of the Future*, trans. Walter Kaufmann (New York: Vintage Books, 1966), 56.

However, one of the key ideas present in Nietzsche's concept of the Übermensch is continual striving. This transcended individual would embrace the challenges and suffering of life, seeing them as opportunities for growth and self-overcoming, forever seeking further advancement. Thus, the Übermensch is still forever entwined with Nietzsche's idea of an endless cycle or eternal recurrence.

This is where my interpretation diverges from earlier philosophies, particularly that of Nietzsche. While Nietzsche conceived of the Will to Power as an eternal force of self-overcoming, refining and creating endlessly for its own sake, I believe this interpretation leaves a crucial question unanswered: Why does this refinement occur in the first place?

My answer lies in the concept of the Asymptrex. The Will to Power strives toward the Asymptrex—a perfected state of existence—first and always. This "perfected state" serves as the guiding principle for the Will to Power's eternal movement, giving it purpose. The endless cycles of culling, refinement, and optimization are driven by this pursuit. Nietzsche's concept of eternal recurrence can be understood as the inevitable result of this striving. Each cycle represents another attempt by the Will to Power to reach perfection, a striving that is never futile, even if it can never be completed.

Even the Übermensch, the transcendent human, continues to long for further refinement and actively pursues it. While the Asymptrex may be unattainable, the Will to Power eternally strives toward it, nonetheless.

Other References

While Nietzsche and Schopenhauer laid the foundation for the Will to Power as a philosophical concept, they were neither the first nor the only great minds to reference this force. Many other thinkers, writers, and cultural works have alluded to the Will to Power—often under different names and, at times, without realizing they were identifying the same phenomenon.

Moore's Law

One such example can be seen in the concept known as "Moore's Law." Gordon Moore, co-founder of Intel, noted that the number of transistors on an integrated circuit was doubling every two years (or, more simply put, that computers were getting noticeably better and faster every two years). This phenomenon was dubbed "Moore's Law."

Its common usage has been expanded to describe the way in which technology improves over time. However, what Moore likely didn't realize was that, in identifying this pattern, he was unknowingly observing the Will to Power in action, moving through and driving the relentless progress of technology.

The Science of Getting Rich

In his work, *The Science of Getting Rich,* Wallace D. Wattles references the Will to Power, although not naming it directly. He writes,

> *"The picture of your desires, held with faith and purpose, is taken up by the Formless, and permeates it through great distances,-- throughout the universe, for all I know. As this impression spreads, all things are set toward its realization; every living thing, every inanimate thing, and the things yet uncreated are stirred toward bringing into being that which you want."*[3]

In this passage, we see Mr. Wattles referencing both the behavior of the Will to Power and what I have termed the Unseen—the realm of all that has yet to exist. He refers to it as "the Formless" and acknowledges the force within it that transforms the uncreated into the created. While he does not name or explicitly identify this force, it is clear that he is describing the Will to Power.

---

[3] Wattles, Wallace D. *The Science of Getting Rich.* Holyoke, MA: Elizabeth Towne, 1910.

Think and Grow Rich

Wallace Wattles was not alone in recognizing how the Will to Power moves through the Unseen to bring about creation. In Napoleon Hill's seminal work, *Think and Grow Rich*, Hill describes this concept as the "cosmic mind."

He suggests that a universal intelligence permeates the universe, serving as the source of human thoughts and inspirations. Hill believed the cosmic mind acts as a medium through which thoughts are transformed into reality. This idea reflects the behavior of the Will to Power as it moves through the Unseen to bring creation into existence.

Taoism

Taoism (or Daoism) is a long-standing religion originating in China. It is believed that Taoism stretches back as far as prehistoric China, but its formal recognition is largely credited with the rise of the work *Daodejing* (Tao Te Ching) between the 6th and 4th century BCE by a man named Laozi.

Taoism describes an ineffable force, the Tao, that governs all things in the cosmos—much like the way I describe the Will to Power. It is believed to flow through all things and is the natural flow of the universe.

Taoism encourages what is called "wu wei" or "effortless action." This does not mean inaction, but rather to live in harmony with the flow of the Tao—to let what is natural be natural. It encourages balance and simplicity—to be like water, strong and adapting, yet capable of overcoming the hardest of obstacles. It also advocates freeing oneself of desire and attachment in order to attain states of peace, balance, and tranquility. While the ideals and guiding principles of Taoism may differ from those suggested by Nietzsche or myself, it is clear that the force being referenced within Taoism is the Will to Power.

As you can see, people have been aware of the Will to Power, even if not directly, for thousands of years. We are in good company in our study of this force.

Keep Going!

If you're still thoroughly confused, don't worry!

While the Will to Power may be a difficult concept to grasp when described by words, it is much easier to understand when you are shown. I have included many examples on the following pages that will show you, without question, the Will to Power moving through existence. Once you're able to identify the Will to Power in *one* thing—to "see it" so to speak—you can and will begin to see it in *everything* else. Remember, there is nothing that the Will to Power does not influence—including you.

The Will to Power in Nature

To begin our study of the Will to Power, we'll start at the most logical of places: nature. In this passage, I'll show you a few examples of the Will to Power moving through nature so you may begin to see it. The study of nature and its history has already produced many terms and ideals that reference the behavior and properties of the Will to Power—despite not identifying it directly. Let's start with the most common term: Evolution.

Evolution

The Mirriam-Webster dictionary defines "evolution" as…

"… the process by which new species or populations of living things develop from preexisting forms through successive generations."

To me, this description describes the behavior of the Will to Power—its ability to cull, refine, and improve upon itself. For this reason, I propose that evolution could also be defined as:

"Observable changes and creation of species within a clade over time as the Will to Power moves through it."

A Single Cell

An example of the Will to Power moving through nature in its most simplistic form can be observed in the process of cellular differentiation during embryonic development.

At the beginning of life, a single fertilized egg divides into identical cells. As development progresses, these cells undergo differentiation, transforming into specialized types such as nerve cells, muscle cells, and skin cells, each with distinct functions. This process is driven by the inherent drive within the cells to organize, specialize, and create increasingly complex structures to form a fully functional organism.

The Will to Power manifests here as the cells' intrinsic force to overcome simplicity and achieve mastery in their roles, constantly refining and improving the organism's structure and functionality. This relentless drive toward complexity and optimization is a perfect embodiment of the Will to Power at the cellular level. It does not explain the biochemical mechanisms behind cell division; rather, it reveals the deeper imperative—the drive toward refinement and continuation. This leads us to a more complex example in the form of modern evolution.

Charles Darwin's Finches

A classic example of evolution comes from none other than Charles Darwin. During a survey voyage in the 1830s aboard the HMS Beagle that included visiting the Galápagos Islands, Darwin collected several species of finches that he later presented to John Gould of the Zoological Society of London.

Due to the difference in physical features of the finches that Darwin collected, he mistakenly misclassified these birds as other, already known species during the voyage. It wasn't until Gould analyzed the specimens in detail that it was discovered that they were, in fact, entirely new species of finch that appeared to have evolved on the islands in different ways due to environmental and dietary needs. This was made apparent by the various forms of beak that developed between the species residing on different islands within the Galápagos. It's believed that these new species emerged from a form of finch that inhabited the island over a million years ago. In the following image, you can see the beak variations that caused Darwin's initial misclassification of these finches.

Finches of the Galápagos Islands. Charles Darwin. Public domain. Image source: Wikimedia Commons.

This discovery by Gould would lead Darwin to his theory of evolution and natural selection. The theory states that organisms within a population that have traits advantageous to their survival are more likely to reproduce and pass these traits on to future generations—ultimately resulting in entirely new species while adapting existing species to their environment. It also states that all species have a common ancestor.

Darwin's theory of evolution and natural selection is a direct observation of the Will to Power and how it moves through, culls, and refines everything in existence. While 'evolution' is the term used and is widely accepted as scientific fact, a deeper analysis reveals that, while not inaccurate, it actually refers to the Will to Power and its behavior. The key difference between evolution and the Will to Power is that evolution primarily describes the process of change in living beings, whereas the Will to Power encompasses all things, both living, non-living, and the intangible—like thought and creativity.

Predator and Prey

The predator-prey dynamic is one of the clearest and most dramatic manifestations of the Will to Power in nature. It drives evolution and refinement across countless species and ecosystems. Just as the Will to Power moved through Darwin's finches and caused them to evolve and refine different physical attributes necessary for survival, it also moves through predators and their prey in a relentless interplay of advancement and counter-advancement.

Consider a cheetah chasing a gazelle on the African savanna. The cheetah, honed by generations of natural selection, sprints with unmatched speed and precision. The gazelle, equally shaped by the forces of evolution, counters with agility and evasive maneuvers. Both creatures strive relentlessly, not out of malice or virtue, but because the force moving through them demands it. This interplay of pursuit and evasion is the Will to Power in action, a testament to the eternal cycle of refinement, adaptation, and optimization.

This push-and-pull manifests across ecosystems at every scale of life. In the oceans, orcas employ coordinated strategies to hunt seals, while the seals develop evasive swimming techniques to survive. Even at the microscopic level, bacteria and viruses engage in a similar struggle, each adapting to outmaneuver the other. In every case, predator and prey continuously refine their abilities, locked in a perpetual cycle of culling and overcoming.

The predator-prey dynamic reflects the Will to Power's relentless striving toward the Asymptrex. While this perfect state may never be attained, it is the striving itself that drives survival, optimization, and the shaping of life as we know it. It is not a story of good versus evil, but a neutral, eternal force moving through and shaping all life.

Homo Habilis to Modern Humans

We can also see the Will to Power when we analyze human evolution. Just as Darwin's finches shared a common ancestor and later evolved into new species, so have humans.

The first of the *Homo* genus from which *Homo sapiens* are believed to have descended is *Homo habilis* or "handy man". This early humanoid variant evolved roughly 2.5 million years ago and is believed to be the first of the *Homo* genus to begin using stone tools.

Following *Homo habilis* was *Homo erectus*. According to fossil records, *Homo erectus* evolved from *Homo habilis* roughly 2 million years ago. This was the first human-like species to have modern human body proportions, exhibiting shorter arms and longer legs for better bipedal movement. It's also believed that *Homo erectus* was the first species of human to use fire and cook food. It is believed that the use of fire led to tremendous changes in behavior and technology that would ultimately result in the rise of modern humans.

Illustration depicting the evolutionary progression of humans from Homo habilis to Homo erectus to Homo sapiens. © 2024 OpenAI.

Using the image above as reference, it's quite easy to see how the Will to Power moved through human biology over time. Going from Homo habilis to Homo sapiens, it refined and optimized our physicality into the form we have today.

While the movement of the Will to Power through human evolution and biology is well-documented within the scientific community, identifying the precise moment and process by which the adoption of technology occurred is far more challenging.

Humans and Fire

It's believed that the control of fire was a key turning point in human evolution. Some of the earliest evidence of humans controlling fire dates back roughly 1 million years. Microscopic traces of ash have been found at archaeological sites, suggesting fire control was in use by *Homo erectus*.[4]

It's likely that fire was discovered by primitive humans as a byproduct of living within nature. Events like lightning strikes and wildfires were naturally occurring phenomena that would have introduced humankind to fire, but it is unclear when the Will to Power moved through this basic understanding of fire taking it from a naturally occurring event to something that could be created by striking flint and pyrite. However, we know it happened, and it is yet another example of the Will to Power moving through all things.

In this case, it was moving through humans' understanding and use of fire. It started as a naturally occurring event that led to humans using fire for warmth, light, and protection. They probably realized quite quickly they could ignite a piece of wood, transport it, and keep it burning. This was probably the first form of fire manipulation by early humans.

Then, our understanding of fire progressed into cooking and environment manipulation—such as burning an area for human habitation, hunting and agriculture. The Will to Power continued to move, leading us to understand fire so well that we began experimenting and eventually learned to manipulate the chemical properties of minerals and stones. This allowed early humans to create heat-treated tools and weaponry. Fast forward to today, and humans' mastery of fire can be seen in the electricity that powers our homes and

---

[4] Francesco Berna et al., "Microstratigraphic Evidence of In Situ Fire in the Acheulean Strata of Wonderwerk Cave, Northern Cape Province, South Africa," *Proceedings of the National Academy of Sciences* 109, no. 20 (2012): E1215–E1220, https://doi.org/10.1073/pnas.1117620109.

devices, much of which is still generated by burning fuels to release energy.

The Emergence of Writing

Equally fascinating as it is mysterious is the birth of writing. How did the Will to Power move through early human communication and bring writing into existence?

While no one knows for certain, it is plausible that the birth of non-biological communication between early humans began when someone decided to draw a shape in the sand to use as a reference to something else. This event was the Will to Power birthing a new form of communication that allowed humans to exchange information in a new way and begin to record history.

Some of the oldest forms of human writing and record keeping are not written words at all, but pictures. A fossilized shell was discovered in Indonesia that dated back roughly 500,000 years. It had zigzag markings that clearly illustrated that *Homo erectus* could and did create imagery.[5] While the meaning of the markings is unknown, it shows that the Will to Power was moving through non-biological human communication much earlier than cave paintings suggest—of which the oldest known paintings are roughly 40,000-50,000 years old.

It is natural to assume that once humans began to communicate using a form of imagery, that the Will to Power would move through this form of communication and further refine it until the first written language would emerge.

The first human writing system is believed to be Sumerian cuneiform, created in early Mesopotamia around 3400 BCE, though some argue that Egyptian hieroglyphics, which emerged around the same time, may have been the earliest. It's believed that both forms of writing developed from an earlier form of proto-writing.

---

[5] Francesco d'Errico et al., "Early Evidence of Engraving on Shells by Homo Erectus," *Nature* 518, no. 7538 (2014): 228–231, https://doi.org/10.1038/nature13962.

We can already see the likely path that the Will to Power took through early writing. It started with a simple shape drawn in the sand, progressed to engravings on a shell, then on to cave paintings and proto-writing, and finally to a recognized system of writing with the emergence of cuneiform and hieroglyphics. In the present day, it is believed that there are currently over 300 writing systems in the world. As the Will to Power continues to move through and refine the written word in all its forms, it's interesting to imagine what writing might look like 500 years from now.

Visualizing the Will to Power

Nature has also supplied us with great aids for visualizing the Will to Power. Have a look at the following close-up picture of a leaf and its veins:

"Green Leaf Texture" by Beeki, licensed under CC BY-SA 4.0, via Wikimedia Commons.

Imagine the leaf is the universe, and that every single vein is the Will to Power moving through a variation of something. This example is quite poignant because it shows that the veins do not move in a linear fashion. There are some obvious paths of progression where the veins are larger and stronger, but many of them move up, down, left, right, and even backward toward their origin point. The Will to Power does not adhere to any preferred direction or path—it simply keeps moving.

Also notice how some of the smaller veins stretch out, bend, and then come to an end. The veins that end are an excellent example of the Will to Power reaching its culmination in something. The Will to Power relentlessly seeks to reach the Asymptrex in all things, even if it leads to the destruction of what it permeates.

A Cosmic Force

Another interesting way to observe the Will to Power in nature is by simply examining what we know about the cosmos. Take, for example, stellar evolution, or put more simply, the life cycle of stars.

A star is created from collapsing clouds of dust and gas. These are referred to as nebulae. Over the course of millions of years, the nebulae collapse in on themselves due to their self-gravity—leading to the formation of protostars. This collapse is not merely a fall into entropy but an act of consolidation and emergence, resulting in the birth of a protostar. In this moment, the Will to Power manifests as a drive toward existence, a striving for energy and heat that ignites nuclear fusion at the core of the star.

Once fusion begins, the star enters its main sequence, the longest and most stable phase of its life. Here, a delicate balance between the force of gravity pulling inward and the outward pressure of fusion energy emerges—an example of the Will to Power in battle with itself. This tension sustains the star, allowing it to generate immense light and heat. Stars in this phase shape their surroundings, nurturing planetary systems and influencing the evolution of life on nearby worlds. Just like the sun being the catalyst for life on Earth. Yet, this equilibrium is temporary, as the star continuously exhausts its nuclear fuel. The drive to sustain itself eventually leads to its transformation into something new. It either expands into a red giant or collapses under its own weight to form a white dwarf.

The death of a star is perhaps the most dramatic expression of the Will to Power. In its final moments, a massive star may explode in a supernova, scattering the elements it forged throughout the cosmos. These elements—carbon, iron, oxygen—become the building blocks of new stars, planets, and even life itself. Through this cycle, the Will to Power moves relentlessly, transforming the ashes of one existence into the foundation of another.

This example perfectly illustrates Nietzsche's concept of eternal recurrence, as well as my interpretation of the Will to Power striving toward the Asymptrex. Since the Asymptrex is forever out of reach of the Will to Power, every star eventually dies, but it does not stop that eternal force from continuing to strive toward perfection by trying again and again.

Conclusion

Through these examples, we've clearly observed how the Will to Power moves through nature. From the simple yet profound drive for expression in cellular division to the grand and constant reshaping of the stars and cosmos, the influence of the Will to Power is absolute and undeniable.

In every aspect of nature, we witness the endless pursuit of perfection—the Asymptrex—by the Will to Power. Recognizing how this force shapes the natural world provides a foundation for understanding its movement through more complex realms, such as human behavior and technology.

The Will to Power in Technology

Now that we've seen some examples of the Will to Power moving through nature, let's study a few examples showing how it moves through non-living entities. We'll begin by looking at how the Will to Power has moved through one of the world's most popular, easily recognizable, and widely used technologies: the smartphone.

Cellular Phones and Smartphones

DynaTAC Phones

The first cellular phone was invented by an engineer at Motorola and debuted in 1973. It was called the DynaTAC 8000X and looked something like the image below.

Image of the Motorola DynaTAC 8000X, the first commercially available mobile phone. © 2006 Rico Shen, licensed under Creative Commons Attribution-ShareAlike 3.0 Unported. Image source: Wikimedia Commons.

As you can see, it was quite large, weighing around 3 pounds. It took roughly 10 hours to charge and offered only 30 minutes of talk time. Its only display was a simple LED screen that would show dialing and recall of roughly 30 numbers. Costing a whopping $4,000 USD in 1984 (equivalent to roughly $12,000 today), this first-generation cell phone was mainly a luxury item for businesses, the wealthy, and techies. I only recall seeing this phone in movies. Not once did I ever see someone using this in public.

Now that we have a starting point, let's analyze how the Will to Power moved through this monstrosity of a phone and into the next generation of cellular devices. First, this was too big and bulky. Second, it offered little in the way of actual talk time since it was limited to roughly 30 minutes. Third, it was expensive. The cost of this technology had to come down if it was to gain mass appeal.

Nokia and Flip Phones

As the Will to Power does, it moves, culls, refines, and optimizes. It did this with the DynaTAC phone and led us to the second generation of cellular phones in the 1990s; most of which resembled the following two models—the Nokia handheld and the Motorola flip phone:

Image of the Motorola v3688 mobile phone. © 2019 Mariusz Stolarz. / Image of the Nokia 6110 mobile phone. © 2018 "Dyna" licensed under Creative Commons Attribution-ShareAlike 4.0 International License. Image source: Wikimedia Commons.

If you grew up during the late 1990s and early 2000s as I did, you remember these two models of cell phones very well. These were the first types of cellular phones to gain mainstream adoption. Let's analyze why.

First, gone was the bulkiness of the past generation of phones; these were now small enough to fit in your pocket. Second, battery life and talk time were drastically improved. Third, these were affordable to the general public, costing only a few hundred or less when purchased with a cellular contract. I vaguely recall purchasing mine for around $100. Fourth, the introduction of SMS (Short Messaging Service) gave birth to texting between mobile devices. Using the small LCD display, one could quickly and easily send and receive text messages (usually at a charge of around 10¢ per text, if you can believe it).

Comparing the two versions, one can quite easily see how the Will to Power moved through the understanding and execution of cellular technology. It culled, optimized, and refined—thus leading to a superior version of the DynaTAC phone.

Blackberry

The next generation of cellular technology came in the form of the Blackberry style of phones in the early/mid 2000s, which looked something like this:

Image of a Blackberry mobile phone. © 2021 Wikimedia Commons user Jeff Cable, licensed under Creative Commons Attribution-ShareAlike 4.0 International License.

The primary improvement found in this model of cellular phone was the inclusion of email services, a larger, more versatile display, and the keyboard interface. The internet's infancy was coming to an end, and the need for internet access and communication was ramping up. While this was a slight improvement over the previous generation of cellular phones, it wasn't quite as popular as its predecessors. However, both would soon be rendered obsolete by the release of the current juggernaut of cellular technology; the smartphone.

Apple iPhone

While not the first smartphone, the Apple iPhone is, without a doubt, the most notable and widely recognizable.

Image of an iPhone. © 2012 Heiko Döring, licensed under Creative Commons Attribution-ShareAlike 3.0 Unported License. Image source: Wikimedia Commons

Introduced in 2007, the Apple iPhone made it clear that this would become the new standard in cell phone technology. Gone were the clumsy keypads and limited LCD screens of the past. We now had touch screen controls on higher resolution displays. Users could also download software (apps) for the device to increase its functionality.

We went from only being able to send and receive calls and texts to being able to talk, text, email, browse the internet, take pictures, and watch or create videos—all on a touchscreen device. In this way, the

Apple iPhone seemed more like a small laptop computer than a cellular phone.

As you can see, the Will to Power made quite a leap through cellular technology in a very short period of time. The smartphone is now so widely adopted by modern society that it has become something of a necessity with nearly all businesses and services using this technology to interact with and service the public.

Conclusion

While it may seem counterintuitive, it's important to remember that this passage is not about the history of cellular phones—it's about the Will to Power. These examples show the nature of the Will to Power and what it does. It moves through, culls, refines, and optimizes, always racing toward the Asymptrex of whatever it is moving through. What started out as a huge, bulky, expensive piece of equipment with only 30 minutes of talk time was quite quickly transformed into a device straight out of science fiction, enabling nearly all forms of modern communication, internet use, and media creation.

One might argue that it is the Will to Power moving through humans that produces these technologies, and they would be correct. However, the evidence of the Will to Power's influence is quite clear when viewing the cellular phone as its own entity. It may not be a living being, but with the aid of humans, the Will to Power moves through it, nevertheless.

Video Games

Let's explore another brief example of the Will to Power moving through technology—this time in the realm of video games. What began as something of a niche hobby in the 1970s has evolved into a multibillion-dollar global industry. We'll begin with the most basic, yet groundbreaking of video games: *Pong*.

Pong

While *Pong* is often credited as the first video game, there were others before it. However, *Pong* was the first game to receive mainstream attention and gain commercial success.

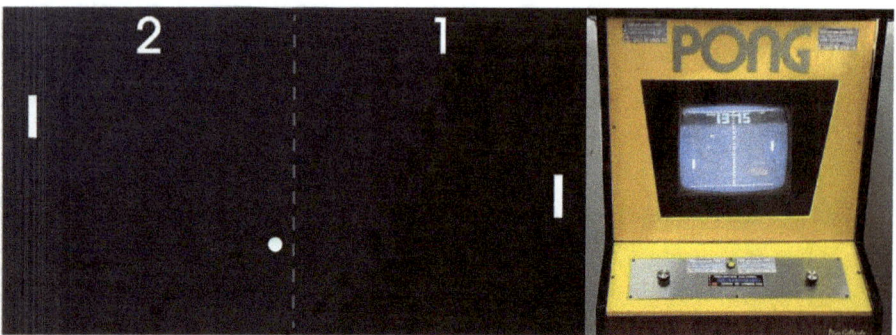

Image of the classic Pong arcade machine. © 2007 Evan-Amos, licensed under Creative Commons Attribution-ShareAlike 3.0 Unported. Image source: Wikimedia Commons.

Manufactured by Atari and released late in 1972, *Pong* was a very simple table tennis game. Upon a black background with white sprites, users adjusted two dials to control the onscreen paddles and bounce the ball back and forth. If the ball made it past one of the paddles, a point would be awarded to the serving player.

It may be hard to believe due to its simplistic nature, but this is the game—combined with the Will to Power—that helped create the gaming industry that we know today. While the arcade cabinet was little more than a television inside of a massive tree trunk, it would only take three years for Atari to release the home version of *Pong* and kick off the epic rise of home video game consoles.

The First Console Wars

Fast forward to the early 1990s and 16-bit gaming is the standard. The original console wars were in full swing with Nintendo and Sega battling it out at every turn.

Images of classic gaming consoles: Sega Mega Drive (Japan Model 1) and Super Nintendo Entertainment System (SNES, Model 1). Both photos © Evan-Amos, licensed under Creative Commons Attribution-ShareAlike 3.0 Unported. Image source: Wikimedia Commons.

While I would love to include screenshots of some of the popular games of the era to illustrate how the Will to Power moved through this period of gaming, copyright and licensing issues prevent me from doing so. In any case, it's not important to see the games to understand that the graphics and gameplay were vastly improved with the consoles of this generation.

These machines brought near-arcade quality sound, music, graphics, and storage to home gaming, allowing players to enjoy an immersive arcade experience without leaving their living rooms. What used to take a dedicated cabinet the size of a vending machine, was now being done by consoles the size of a VCR. The Will to Power continued driving the gaming industry forward; and like cellular phones, consoles steadily evolved and improved.

This progress continued and eventually the Super Nintendo and the Sega Genesis were replaced by the current juggernauts of the home gaming industry: Playstation and Xbox. Graphics, sound, gameplay, storylines, and everything in between continued to feel the influence of the Will to Power and improve at an impressive rate. This led us to near life-like graphics and lightning-fast gameplay. The following screenshot shows how much the Will to Power changed gaming on a graphical level from *Pong*:

Screenshot from War of the Vikings. © 2013 Fatshark, licensed under Creative Commons Attribution-ShareAlike 3.0 Unported. Image source: Wikimedia Commons.

Depending on how you're viewing this book, the above screenshot may or may not be that impressive. However, seeing the fine details of the screenshot is not important. It's simply an example showing how the Will to Power has moved through this medium in its relentless push toward the Asymptrex and perfection—resulting in near photorealistic graphics in video games.

Graphical and computational improvements are not the only way the Will to Power moves through the medium of gaming. In fact, a very interesting way to see this force in action is to look at what kind of actions take place within a given video game. Almost all video games are Will to Power-oriented in their gameplay. Meaning that in many instances, your video game character will start out relatively weak. As you perform tasks and play the game, you may gain levels, equipment, and abilities that make your character stronger. This style of gameplay is a direct manifestation of the Will to Power. Just as this force moves through us in real life and we seek improvement and self-mastery, it is also something we crave in this form of entertainment—or, put more accurately, it is why we find it entertaining in the first place.

Multiplayer and open-world games are also excellent examples of how the Will to Power moves through both humans and gaming. In these types of games, the desire for self-mastery, exploration, dominance, competition, and cooperation are front and center—mirroring the drive that moves humanity in the real world. As the Will to Power races through humans, we constantly strive to seek out new frontiers and challenges so that we continue to overcome obstacles and grow, just as we do in our video games.

Conclusion

In the realm of video games, the Will to Power is both a driving force and a reflection of humanity's ceaseless striving for mastery and self-overcoming. From the simplistic paddles of *Pong* to the immersive, photorealistic worlds of modern gaming, we see the relentless movement of this force. Not just in the technology itself but in the players who inhabit these virtual spaces. By understanding how the Will to Power manifests in this medium, we gain not only insight into the evolution of gaming but also a deeper understanding of how this force shapes every aspect of human ambition and creativity.

How it Started versus How it's Going

I wanted to include a few more brief examples of the Will to Power moving through technology but without the superfluous technical analysis. Here are a few more illustrations of how the Will to Power has moved through some of the more popular technologies that we use every day.

Televisions

How it started:

"Old Television Set" by Evan-Amos is licensed under CC0 1.0 (Public Domain). Available at Wikimedia Commons: Old Television Set.

How it's going:

Image courtesy of www.freeimageslive.co.uk, licensed by www.freeimages.co.uk. For full license details, visit www.freeimageslive.co.uk. Credit: www.freeimageslive.co.uk / gratuit.

We went from huge, bulky RCA TVs to slim, sleek flat-screen TVs.

Clothes Washer

How it started:

"Kids learn about life on the wagon trail during the California Trail Interpretive Center grand opening" by the Bureau of Land Management, available under CC BY 2.0. Source: Wikimedia Commons.

How it's going:

"The Twins - Matag washer and dryer" by Joe Mabel is licensed under CC BY-SA 3.0. Source: Wikimedia Commons.

We went from a washboard and bucket to modern washing and drying units.

Vehicles

How it started:

Coachmen with Horse and Carriage, Havana, Cuba, 1830s-1840s. Public domain image courtesy of Wikimedia Commons

How it's going:

VW I.D. Buggy at the Geneva Motor Show, 2019. © Alexander Migl, licensed under CC BY-SA 4.0, via Wikimedia Commons.

We went from a horse-drawn carriage to a modern electric vehicle.

Conclusion

The examples shared here demonstrate how the Will to Power moves through each area of technology as its own evolving entity. Through culling, refining, and optimizing, this relentless force drives technological progression, always striving toward the Asymptrex in an unending quest for perfection.

The Will to Power in Humans

We've explored how the Will to Power moves through nature and inanimate entities like technology. Now we'll look at how the Will to Power moves through humans. This isn't a passage that continues exploring the biological evolution of humans, but rather one that explores how the Will to Power moves through humans and manifests itself through our thoughts, behaviors, actions, and habits.

"Good" and "Bad" do not Apply

The first thing we need to bring to the forefront of this conversation is that the Will to Power does not distinguish between good and bad behaviors or outcomes—it simply wishes to reach its point of completion and perfection. This aspect of the Will to Power is extremely important in regard to the way it manifests and moves through humans because it can lead to outcomes in which an individual thrives and achieves, just the same as it can lead to outcomes in which the individual masters self-destructive habits that ultimately lead to a life of struggle, misery, and eventually death.

For every social media influencer who strives to bring joy and entertainment to the world, there is another who is using the same approach to sow seeds of fear and hate. For every humanitarian pushing themselves to make the world a better place for all, there is another who seeks only power, control, and subjugation for individual gain. For every student who spends years mastering good study habits and work ethic, there is someone who develops habits and mastery over a life of substance abuse—often to their detriment.

The Will to Power is the reason for the height of human achievement and success while simultaneously being the reason for the absolute lowest depths of human depravity and destruction. The Will to Power is neutral and unbiased, but forever moving, culling, optimizing, and perfecting.

Habits: Reflections of the Will to Power

If you want to see how the Will to Power has manifested and moved through your life thus far, one need look no further than one's own habits. Everyone, without exception, has and develops habits. Habits reflect how you have consciously or unconsciously allowed the Will to Power to move through and shape your life.

What is a "habit"? It is a thought, behavior or action that one does with regularity and requires little conscious thought or effort. For example, how many of you reading this wake up in the morning and the very first thing you do, without even thinking about it, is grab your smartphone?

Habits are something of a "cheat code" for the Will to Power. It's quite inefficient to make a creature experience everything as though it were happening for the first time, regardless of how many times something may have been experienced. Habits eliminate this problem and allow the Will to Power to move through a being much more efficiently. An excellent example of this can be seen in the phenomena of muscle memory. Humans and animals can do a physical task so frequently that the Will to Power basically says, "You no longer need conscious thought to perform this action."

Take an expert guitarist, for example. The guitarist who has played for 30 years no longer needs to look at their fingers to align with the correct frets when strumming a chord. Nor do they need to think about the motion or positioning of their hand when going from an A-note to a C-note—their muscle memory takes over. Muscle memory could be described as the physical manifestation of habit.

While all creatures in nature exhibit habits, humans are somewhat unique in that we maintain a level of intelligence and self-awareness that allows us to identify, create, and change our habits. If habits are a reflection of the Will to Power, and we can cultivate or change our habits, then it must also mean that we have the ability to influence how the Will to Power flows through our lives. This realization—that human intent can influence the flow and manifestation of the Will to

Power—is an understanding that is paramount for the success of not just the individual, but for humanity as a whole.

We'll dive more into how one can use their understanding of the Will to Power to cultivate desirable habits later in this book. For now, it's enough to know that habits exist as a reflection of the force itself. At this point, I encourage you to take stock of your own habits. What habits do you currently have that you have cultivated consciously or unconsciously? How has the Will to Power moved through the formation and refinement of these habits over time?

Perhaps one morning, you decided to treat yourself to an expensive cup of coffee on your way to work. One year later, you find yourself stopping by that same coffee shop every single workday. Or perhaps you went to the gym with a group of friends one afternoon. One year later, you find yourself going multiple times a week—with or without them. Or perhaps, after a particularly stressful day, you poured yourself a glass of wine while preparing dinner. Now, one year later, that single glass during dinner has turned into finishing an entire bottle every night.

Whether we're conscious of it or not, the Will to Power continuously moves through and refines our habits—both good and bad. It's the conscious understanding of this truth that gives an individual agency over the Will to Power itself.

8 Billion Minds and Counting

At the time of this writing, it is estimated that there are roughly eight billion humans on Earth. That is eight billion unique minds and eight billion unique avenues that the Will to Power will travel through. This leads to some interesting and terrifying realizations when viewed through a lens of the same force. Nearly every facet of life that can be imagined will be explored by someone.

I found an interesting example of this when I stumbled upon the video game speedrunning community. It may sound odd, but for just about every video game you can think of, no matter how old or obscure, there is a community behind it that devotes countless hours in pursuit of mastering that game and completing it in the fastest possible time.

Thanks to talented content producers on YouTube like Karl Jobst and Summoning Salt, I was able to see and analyze how the Will to Power moves through this hobby and those that enjoy it. Karl Jobst creates speedrunning analysis videos, specializing in uncovering and exposing cheaters within the speedrunning and video game community. Summoning Salt, on the other hand, produces excellent documentary-style videos that chronicle the history of world record progression for various popular speedrunning games. Summoning Salt's videos, in particular, offer a fascinating way to view how the Will to Power moves through this hobby, as he explores individual runners, evolving strategies, and the techniques that push records to ever-increasing heights.

At first, I thought it quite strange that there were people putting in such amazing amounts of time, effort, and energy to be ranked number one for speedrunning a video game—particularly a game that may not even be popular outside of the niche audience that participates in speedrunning it. In many instances, these players aren't attempting to achieve the top ranking for monetary gain or mainstream notoriety as there is none to be had—they are doing it for the love of the game and the hobby itself.

A prime example of one such speedrunner is Arcus, who achieved multiple world records for the Nintendo game *Ninja Gaiden*. This player racked up an astounding 27,000 attempts over years and hundreds of hours of gameplay—an excellent example of the Will to Power striving for perfection through an individual.

It was in studying the speedrunning community and the almost obsessive nature of the hobby that I began to truly grasp the scope of the Will to Power in humanity. In every single facet and discipline in life, no matter how niche or obscure, there will always be someone at the pinnacle of it.

While the Will to Power can inspire remarkable dedication and creativity, the same relentless force also propels individuals toward darker pursuits, revealing the dual and unbiased nature of the Will to Power. For every individual who ascends to the pinnacle of their discipline—whether it's a speedrunner breaking a long-standing record or a scientist unraveling nature's secrets—there is another who channels the same drive toward destruction, such as a serial killer perfecting their heinous craft or an engineer making a more powerful nuclear weapon. The Will to Power is the same; it is the direction that differs. This dual nature brings to light some disturbing conclusions about the manifestation of immoral acts—like cheating.

If it can be Cheated, it will be Cheated

Another interesting realization I came to during my study of the Will to Power moving through the speedrunning community was that if it can be cheated, it will be cheated.

Karl Jobst has produced many excellent videos that bring cheating activities to light within the speedrunning and video game community. In reviewing these videos, what surprised me the most was the lengths that some of these players would go to in their attempts to cheat the community and leaderboards associated with whatever game they were playing. Some of these cons would span several years and hundreds of hours of time and effort.

You might assume that most of the cheaters exposed were simply bad players who used cheating to gain an edge they wouldn't have been able to acquire through diligent practice, but you would be incorrect. In many instances, the players who were caught cheating were actually very proficient within their game of choice—some even exhibiting top-level skill and talent while being very active and respected within their communities. This paradox—where even the highly skilled feel compelled to cheat—highlights how the Will to Power is not satisfied with proficiency alone but seeks absolute dominance and perfection, even at the cost of integrity.

The interesting part of researching such cheating was that while some were cheating due to monetary incentives like growing their streaming audience or acquiring sponsorship deals, others were going to the same, if not greater lengths, when there was little or no monetary gain to be had. Many were simply doing it to gain notoriety in their community, however niche it was, and simply because they could.

While the speedrunning community offers a fascinating lens through which to observe cheating manifesting as an expression of the Will to Power, the behaviors observed within it are not isolated; they echo patterns found throughout all human competition and interaction. For example, take business scandals like Enron and Theranos—two infamous cases of cheating in business.

Enron engaged in massive accounting fraud by hiding debts and inflating profits through off-the-books entities. This created a false image of financial health, misleading investors and employees, ultimately leading to its collapse and widespread economic harm.

Theranos falsely claimed its technology could perform a wide array of blood tests with just a small sample. The company manipulated test results, deceived regulators and partners, and endangered patient health, all to maintain its facade of innovation to deceive investors and the public into believing in a technology that never delivered on its promises.

It's important to keep in mind that cheating extends beyond gaming and corporate scandals. It also extends to politics, academia, and even personal relationships. It's this type of dishonest behavior that explicitly shows the unbiased nature of the Will to Power and how it will manifest in every avenue imaginable. This isn't to say that every person is a cheater, far from it. It is simply saying that if it can be cheated, it will be cheated by someone somewhere—the Will to Power's unending and unbiased manifestation ensures this.

Thoughts are Things

Since we know that the Will to Power moves through all things, it is important to note that human thoughts are no exception. A single, fleeting thought, seemingly insignificant, has the potential to spawn an entire identity for an individual. This subject has been touched upon in other philosophical works and is usually identified as "The Law of Attraction." It states that positive thoughts and actions produce positive results, while negative thoughts and actions produce negative results.

I would respectfully argue that it is not simply a matter of like attracting like but instead, it is the Will to Power moving through thoughts—thus creating patterns of thought that eventually manifest as behaviors and habits.

This can be seen in countless ways, but one of the most poignant examples I can think of is in individuals that suffer from body dysmorphia—a mental disorder in which a person is obsessively critical about their physical appearance. When viewing this disorder through a lens of the Will to Power, it becomes quite easy to see how an individual could develop such an illness.

What may start out as a singular thought of "I don't think I'm good looking" can evolve into an all-encompassing narrative: "I'm not thin enough. My nose is too big. My skin is gross. My eyes are too narrow." As the Will to Power moves through these thoughts, it refines and expands them, making them more extreme over time. These refined thought patterns eventually manifest as behaviors and habits, such as skipping meals, which itself may be further refined and optimized, becoming full-blown anorexia.

It is important to remember that the Will to Power will also move through thoughts of empowerment and self-improvement. "I'm a good person" can lead one to a personal narrative like: "I try to treat others with kindness. I'm patient when people make mistakes. I actively look for ways to help those in need. I'm making a positive difference in the lives of others." Just as in the previous example, the Will to Power will move through and refine these thoughts, develop them into patterns of thinking, and ultimately manifest as behaviors and habits.

This means one must exercise agency over their own mind lest the Will to Power be allowed to run rampant like a fire burning indiscriminately through a forest. While controlling one's thoughts sounds like a daunting task, the beauty of understanding the Will to Power is that we know we don't need a million positive thoughts to begin creating the patterns of thought we desire—we need only one. To have and focus intentionally on a singular thought is to ignite the Will to Power's movement through and refinement of it.

Relationships: Humans with Humans

With the Will to Power coursing uniquely through every individual, analyzing humanity's collective behavior through its lens can be quite challenging. Humans like to believe that we are so intelligent and unique that the common instinctual manifestations of the Will to Power within the animal kingdom do not apply to us—but that couldn't be further from the truth. It's this hubris and unwillingness to view ourselves as primal beings that create many conflicts and misunderstandings in human relationships.

The truth is that beneath the layers of culture, intellect, and morality, humans are driven by the same primal forces that guide all life. The Will to Power moves through us as it does through a pride of lions or a colony of ants, shaping our behavior and interactions in ways that define our relationship to the broader community. Whether we are nurturing a child, competing for resources, or striving for recognition, this force drives us to assert, expand, and refine ourselves in relation to others.

It's important to strip away our own hubris if we are to analyze how the Will to Power moves through humanity as a species. While we may be the most advanced beings on the planet, we are not so unique that commonalities between humans and animals do not exist.

Just like all lifeforms in existence, humans have an innate desire and drive to reproduce. This yearning for procreation is one of the purest expressions of the Will to Power while simultaneously being one of the most powerful. While the individual motivations for reproduction may differ from person to person, it is the Will to Power that is the core force behind our desire to propagate our species. In this regard, we are no different than the lions of the Serengeti or the salmon of the Atlantic.

The Will to Power doesn't end upon the act of reproduction, however. It continues seamlessly into the relationship that is immediate between parent and offspring—with the Will to Power coursing through both, driving their interactions and shaping their bond.

Parent and Child

Parents, compelled by the Will to Power, strive to protect, teach, and mold their children, seeking to extend their own legacy and ideals through the success of the next generation. This is not merely a biological imperative but a reflection of the Will to Power's drive for continuity and refinement.

Children, on the other hand, are equally moved by the Will to Power in their relentless quest for autonomy and self-expression. From the moment they learn to say "no," they begin asserting their individuality, testing boundaries, and seeking mastery over their environment. This interplay between parental guidance and a child's growing independence creates a dynamic that is both cooperative and adversarial—a microcosm of the Will to Power in action.

As children grow and mature, the balance of power shifts. Adolescence, often characterized by rebellion and self-discovery, marks a period where the Will to Power moves through individuals most visibly. The tension between parents' desire to guide and a teenager's push for freedom is a natural outgrowth of this force striving for expression in the family dynamic.

It's this power struggle between parent and child, with the Will to Power being the driving force of both, that can create the most challenging and sometimes damaging interactions. Adolescents, propelled by their growing independence, seek to test limits and assert their individuality, often clashing with parents who feel a deep responsibility to protect and guide. The result is a dynamic where both parties are striving for mastery and dominance—parents over the shaping of their child's future, and children over their own burgeoning sense of self.

This tension is not inherently negative however. It is, in many ways, a necessary stage of development for both sides. For parents, it represents an opportunity to adapt and refine their approach to nurturing, transitioning from direct authority to supportive guidance. For adolescents, it provides the fertile ground needed to grow into autonomous individuals capable of navigating the complexities of adulthood. The friction, while often uncomfortable, serves as a crucible for growth, with the Will to Power driving each party toward their respective goals.

When this process is approached with an understanding of the Will to Power and the desires it is manifesting, the parent-child relationship can evolve into one of mutual respect and collaboration. These unique desires and drives, instead of being a source of conflict, become a venue of expression for the Will to Power that fosters growth and strengthens the bond.

Conversely, when the struggle is marked by rigidity or a refusal to adapt by one or both parties, the result can be estrangement or lingering resentment. In such cases, the unchecked drive of the Will to Power, left without a constructive outlet or common understanding between parent and child, can damage what might otherwise have been a deeply fulfilling relationship. After all, the Will to Power does not prefer one outcome over the other—it simply moves, manifesting and expressing itself, refining the parent-child relationship into whatever it will become as it is guided by the conscious or unconscious behavior of both parent and child.

Interpersonal Relationships

Just as the Will to Power moves through and refines the parent-child relationship, so too does it flow through and shape our relationships with others outside of the family dynamic. From the classroom to the boardroom, this force plays an integral part in how we interact with one another in forming friendships, rivalries, collaborations, and even romantic partnerships. Let's examine how the Will to Power manifests in a group setting. We'll start with an example from nature: the pecking order of chickens.

When chickens are thrown together in a group, a natural hierarchy emerges. This hierarchy is referred to as the "pecking order." The pecking order dictates the dynamics of dominance and submission within the group, determining which chickens have priority access to resources such as food, water, and shelter. Those at the top of the hierarchy assert their dominance through displays of aggression or confidence, while those lower in the order acquiesce to avoid conflict. This natural social structure reflects the Will to Power in action, as each chicken instinctively strives to assert its position within the group, driven by the innate need to secure resources and ensure survival.

You can see this same type of social dynamic emerge in other species as well, such as wolves or primates, where hierarchies are established through displays of strength, dominance, or submission. Despite our intelligence and hubris, humans are no different. If you take a group of humans and put them together, the Will to Power manifests in much the same way, and a social hierarchy will naturally emerge.

Take, for example, a classroom of young students on the first day of school. If we assume that the students are all meeting one another for the first time and are beginning the school year with no preset form of social dynamics within the group, over the course of the school year, the Will to Power will move through the students and a natural hierarchy and social structure will emerge among them.

Some students may assert themselves as leaders, driven by charisma, confidence, or a natural inclination toward taking charge. Others may take on supportive roles, aligning themselves with stronger personalities to gain social security or acceptance. Meanwhile, some may find themselves on the periphery, either by choice or by being excluded from the dominant social groups. These roles are not static; as the Will to Power moves through the students individually, shifts in the social hierarchy can occur, driven by changing circumstances, personal growth, or new opportunities to assert influence.

One can observe this same manifestation of the Will to Power in workplace settings as well. Even in environments where job titles and responsibilities are uniform, the Will to Power ensures that informal hierarchies form based on factors like personality, competence, social influence, or even physical presence. Employees may assert dominance by excelling in tasks, garnering the favor of leadership, or rallying colleagues to their perspectives. Others may adopt more passive or collaborative roles, seeking harmony over conflict—just as in the animal kingdom.

This interplay can create tension when the informal hierarchy clashes with the official structure, such as when a subordinate gains more influence over the group than their manager or when leadership struggles to assert authority over dominant personalities within the team. These conflicts are not merely the result of human ambition but a direct manifestation of the Will to Power driving individuals to assert, refine, and optimize their own positions within the workplace dynamic.

Understanding this movement can provide valuable insight for leaders and employees alike. By recognizing the natural tendencies of the Will to Power within the workplace, individuals can better navigate these dynamics, fostering cooperation and productivity rather than allowing conflict to derail progress. Moreover, being conscious of the Will to Power offers a unique advantage—it allows one to influence its flow and manifestation within the group, whether a manager or employee.

For instance, a manager aware of the Will to Power can identify emerging informal leaders within their team and channel their influence toward productive collaboration, preventing potential power struggles and fostering a more cohesive work environment. Conversely, an employee aware of the Will to Power can recognize the informal dynamics shaping their workplace, allowing them to align with influential colleagues or position themselves as a valuable contributor. This awareness helps them navigate challenges, build strategic relationships, and increase their influence without direct authority.

Whether in the boss-employee dynamic, the parent-child relationship, or the predator-prey fight for survival, the underlying force remains the same: the Will to Power drives each party to assert, adapt, and refine their position, creating a constant interplay of dominance, submission, and evolution that shapes the dynamics of every relationship.

A Wider View

If the same force underpins these individual and small-group dynamics, it stands to reason that the Will to Power would manifest similarly when we scale up our perspective. What happens when we observe its influence across a larger collective, such as a country like the United States?

Just as in the smaller collectives, we see the emergence of both leaders and followers. In the case of a country, we see this emergence in the form of city, state and federal governmental agencies. Each has their own internal set of leaders and followers. These layers of governance are not static; they are dynamic ecosystems shaped by competition, collaboration, and conflict—all manifestations of the Will to Power. Within them, individuals and groups strive to assert influence, secure resources, and implement visions of what the nation should become.

This ongoing interplay within governance is the Will to Power at work, and can be seen most notably during political campaigns where politicians attempt to rally supporters while vilifying their opponents. Similar to the prior predator-prey example, this back-and-forth rhetoric between candidates serves as the battlefield through which the Will to Power moves through and refines the public's perception of the political landscape based on the individual ideals, goals, and policies of each candidate.

However, as with all human systems, the political landscape is not immune to the darker side of the Will to Power. The maxim "if it can be cheated, it will be cheated" holds particularly true in this realm, where the stakes are highest, and the rewards of dominance are immense. This drive leads to the manipulation of electoral processes, the spreading of misinformation, and the exploitation of legal loopholes to maintain or gain power. In this case, the Will to Power, moving through individuals and groups, does not distinguish between ethical and unethical means; it seeks only to achieve its end by manifesting through the corrupt, racing toward the Asymptrex at the expense of fairness and trust in the system.

Instances of gerrymandering, voter suppression, and campaign finance loopholes are examples of this principle in action. Political entities use these tools not necessarily out of intended malice but as unconscious (or perhaps conscious) expressions of the Will to Power's neutral, relentless drive to dominate and optimize their own position. Even within democratic systems designed to ensure equality and fairness, this force finds ways to manifest through exploitation of vulnerabilities, revealing the universal truth that the Will to Power will manifest in every possible form— ethical or unethical.

This dynamic has profound consequences for society. While the relentless striving of the Will to Power can lead to progress and reform, its ability to manifest as corruption also erodes public trust and fuels cynicism. Recognizing the presence of this force in the political sphere is essential not only to understanding the system's flaws but also to addressing them. By acknowledging the inevitability of such manifestations of the Will to Power, we can strive to create mechanisms that channel this force toward constructive outcomes while mitigating its potential for harm.

Again, humanity should not rely on systems of election and governance where human agency is the primary factor in ensuring the system's integrity. Because we know that the Will to Power will manifest through any and every venue of expression, it's imperative that our political systems reflect this by exhibiting the upmost level of transparency and authenticity. We should not design systems that discourage humans from trying to cheat them; we should design systems whose core purpose is to make it as difficult as possible for the Will to Power to manifest in negative ways—such as corruption and cheating.

Economic systems further highlight the Will to Power's influence in a national context. Capitalism, for instance, thrives on competition and innovation, both of which are driven by this force. Entrepreneurs race to create new products, gain market dominance, and redefine industries. However, just as in the natural world, this striving for power can also lead to monopolies and imbalances, where dominant entities suppress or extinguish competition and consolidate control—a reflection of the Will to Power's dual nature of creation and destruction.

Capitalism vividly demonstrates the inherent nature of the Will to Power on a global scale. Its influence extends far beyond America, shaping the world at large as resources, power, and wealth are continually concentrated in the hands of a select few individuals and entities. It's in this continual act of consolidation that one can plainly see the Will to Power racing through capitalism toward the Asymptrex.

Cultural movements within a nation are yet another domain where the Will to Power is evident. Artists, activists, and thinkers seek to influence public consciousness, often challenging existing norms to reshape society in their image. Whether through protest, art, or literature, these individuals and groups channel the force to create ripples of change that may eventually become tsunamis of transformation.

One need look no further than the sordid history of slavery in America for proof of such change being possible. The fact that this practice was abolished shows that subjugation is not final as long as the Will to Power exists—and it is in this challenging and overcoming of established order that is the essence of the force itself.

Finally, international relations showcase the Will to Power on the grandest stage. Nations compete for dominance through economic strategies, military advancements, and alliances. The pursuit of geopolitical influence, whether through soft power like cultural diplomacy or hard power like military interventions, demonstrates the universal reach of this force. This means that no matter how large the scale, the Will to Power's influence is the same.

When viewed through the lens of the Will to Power, the story of a nation becomes one of constant striving—within its borders and beyond. Leaders rise and fall, ideologies emerge and fade, and societies continually refine themselves in the relentless pursuit of the Asymptrex—or in this context, the perfect society.

Friendships

It may seem like an odd question, but why do humans seek the companionship of other humans? When viewed through a lens of the Will to Power, the need for companionship may seem to stem from hundreds of thousands of years of evolutionary instinct. It would have been advantageous for early humans to seek out one another to increase their chances of survival in harsh environments by sharing resources and responsibilities.

It is within these early cooperative bonds that the Will to Power first manifests in human companionship, driving individuals to form alliances that optimize their ability to survive and thrive. This same dynamic can be viewed when analyzing other social creatures within the animal kingdom, like chimpanzees or wolf packs—where friendships and alliances are clearly visible within the groups. This instinctual need for connection, initially born out of necessity, becomes yet another avenue of expression for the Will to Power.

Through these relationships, humans derive meaning—affirming, asserting, and expanding their sense of self in relation to others. They gravitate toward companions who share their values, goals, and interests, creating bonds that affirm and strengthen their perspectives on the world.

Friendships also provide fertile ground for personal growth and self-discovery. By interacting with others who not only share but challenge their perspectives, individuals refine their understanding of themselves and each other. The Will to Power moves through these relationships of mutual growth, pushing both parties toward a greater realization of their potential.

This interplay is not without complexity. Even the most genuine friendships harbor subtle power dynamics. Through influence, collaboration, or occasional rivalry, companions negotiate roles and assert themselves within the relationship. In close-knit groups of friends, we observe the same manifestations of the Will to Power as in other human group dynamics, where dominant and submissive roles naturally emerge. Even in a friendship between two individuals, the Will to Power ensures that one person often assumes a dominant role, shaping the terms and direction of the relationship.

These emergent power dynamics are not inherently negative, as they serve as a crucible for individual growth where all parties, dominant and submissive, continuously refine their identities and roles within the relationship. The dominant figure may gain leadership skills and learn to express subservience through interaction with the submissive, while the submissive figure learns assertiveness and resilience under the protection or guidance of the dominant figure. This give-and-take within friendships perfectly illustrates the Will to Power's continued movement through and refinement of both the individuals and the relationship itself.

Conversely, while the Will to Power can refine a friendship toward mutual growth and self-discovery, it can also manifest destructively. Take, for example, a pair of friends in which each amplifies and encourages the destructive behaviors or habits in the other—such as drug or alcohol abuse. Instead of the Will to Power optimizing and refining the relationship toward individual growth, it optimizes and refines it toward mutual destruction.

This type of destructive manifestation can also take the form of exploitative or competitive dynamics, where an individual consistently takes more from the relationship than they contribute. This type of dynamic can be seen most notably in modern parasocial relationships that develop between influential figures and the fan bases they cultivate.

In a world where online discourse is increasingly taking the place of face-to-face interaction, the inherent drive for community and companionship is not made irrelevant. Instead, this drive finds new avenues of expression in the digital age, where the Will to Power manifests through one-sided relationships between influential figures and their audiences. Parasocial relationships, by definition, are imbalanced connections in which one party—a public figure, influencer, or content creator—becomes an object of emotional investment and attachment for the other party, often without reciprocation or direct interaction.

In these relationships, the Will to Power moves asymmetrically. The influential figure refines their identity and builds their platform through the adoration and loyalty of their fan base, while the fans continually project their desires, values, and aspirations onto someone they admire from a distance.

For the influencer, this dynamic offers a clear avenue for self-assertion and growth, as their reach and influence expand through the collective energy of their audience. For the fans, however, this relationship often attempts to fulfill emotional or psychological needs, such as belonging, inspiration, or a sense of connection, without the mutuality found in traditional friendships. This disparity reflects the inherent imbalance of parasocial relationships, where one party benefits disproportionately from the dynamic, while the other derives meaning from a connection that may ultimately be illusory. Streaming and Influencer culture serve as a pristine example of the Will to Power manifesting in a way that strives to meet the human drive for companionship in a world that is increasingly devoid of traditional, face-to-face forms of interaction.

Romantic Relationships

Understanding how the Will to Power moves through and manifests within interpersonal relationships gives us a foundation from which we can begin to analyze how this force manifests through one of the most complex forms of human interaction: romantic relationships.

As we did in prior examples, we'll start our analysis at the beginning by looking at the core components that govern romantic relationships. As stated earlier, the drive to reproduce is an extremely powerful expression of the Will to Power. When viewing humanity as a subject of pure analysis, it seems logical to conclude that this inherent drive serves as the basis for the formation of romantic relationships.

Using this basis as our starting point, we can begin to understand mate selection among humans. The most powerful and initial aspect of mate selection comes in the form of physical attraction.

Physical attraction, at its core, is a manifestation of the Will to Power as it seeks to optimize and refine the human species. Traits considered physically appealing often serve as subconscious indicators of health, vitality, and genetic fitness. Symmetry, clear skin, and physical fitness are universally recognized markers that signal an individual's ability to thrive and pass on favorable genetic traits to future generations. These attributes are not random preferences but deeply ingrained instincts, shaped by the Will to Power over thousands of years of evolutionary pressures.

In women, this often manifests as physical cues of health and fertility, such as clear skin, a youthful appearance, and body proportions associated with reproductive health, like a waist-to-hip ratio that signals optimal childbearing potential. These traits have been biologically ingrained as markers of vitality, signaling to potential mates the ability to conceive and raise offspring successfully.

In men, the Will to Power often manifests as physical traits that signal strength, vitality, and genetic fitness—qualities that suggest an ability to protect and provide. Broad shoulders, a muscular build, and a strong, angular jawline are frequently considered attractive because they convey an ability to hunt, protect, and secure resources in ancestral environments where physical prowess was essential for survival. Deep voices and facial symmetry are also physical attributes associated with high testosterone levels, further emphasizing perceived genetic fitness. These characteristics subtly communicate to potential mates that an individual possesses the strength and resilience needed to endure and thrive in challenging environments. The Will to Power moves through these traits, optimizing physical indicators to align with reproductive success and the broader goals of survival and refinement.

Take, for example, six-pack abs in males. This physical trait has become a contemporary symbol of fitness and discipline. From the perspective of potential mates, it signals strength, stamina, and endurance—qualities linked to reproductive success. The Will to Power uses traits like six-pack abs as avenues of refinement within the human physique to not only convey genetic health, but to enhance an individual's perceived desirability. Moreover, in modern contexts, six-pack abs also reflect the discipline and resources required to achieve such a physique, subtly indicating mental fortitude and economic stability, which further enhances their appeal.

It's also important to note that these physical cues are not limited to heterosexual relationships. In same-sex relationships, these indicators of health and vitality continue to play a significant role in shaping physical attraction, serving as universal markers of genetic fitness and appeal.

Humanity has long been aware of these physical indicators as a means of attraction. This is why we often see these traits exaggerated when expressed in modern media and art. The portrayal of the female form often exhibits an exaggerated bust, shapely hips, and full buttocks. Whereas the male portrayal exaggerates features like a broad, muscular upper body, a flat, chiseled stomach, and well-defined chest and jawline.

The use of makeup and cosmetic surgery also serves as proof of humanity's awareness of these physical cues of attraction. Makeup serves as a tool to amplify and accent the subtle facial indicators that signal genetic health and fitness—such as full lips and smooth skin. Likewise, cosmetic surgery is often used to create or enhance facial symmetry and body proportions that convey the same physical message.

While these observations of common physical attraction markers may hold true when viewing humanity as a whole, they carry less weight when the focus shifts to smaller groups or individuals. Physical attraction preferences can vary wildly when narrowed to the personal level. The Will to Power moves through and refines each of us in uniquely profound ways, meaning that for some, traditionally attractive physical attributes may hold little appeal, while other, less conventional traits resonate deeply.

These personal preferences can be influenced by any number of factors—such as past romantic partners, past experiences with the opposite sex, influential figures throughout one's life, and instances of trauma. Any or all of these can serve as influencing factors that are ultimately refined by the Will to Power within the individual and manifest as a preference in regard to physical attraction. This diversity of preference is what gives rise to the idea of "types." Anytime you've thought or said, "They are exactly my type!" you were unknowingly acknowledging how the Will to Power has shaped and refined your individual sense of physical attraction.

Beyond physical attraction lies everything else—personality, emotional maturity, intelligence, humor, measurements of societal and professional success, and every other nuanced measurement one can think of—all of which help to serve as indicators of compatibility and attraction in mate selection.

For women evaluating partners, non-physical traits of attraction often include qualities like intelligence, humor, personality, and professional success—an attribute that signals a potential mate's discipline and ability to provide for and protect her and future offspring. While modern society may sometimes label this evaluation as "shallow," it is important to recognize that this metric of mate selection has been shaped and refined over hundreds of thousands of years. Throughout history, particularly during the evolutionary period spanning *Homo habilis* to *Homo sapiens*, the vulnerability associated with pregnancy and child-rearing often posed life-threatening risks. In such contexts, a woman's ability to accurately assess a mate's ability to provide and protect—from not only nature and famine, but other humans—could literally mean the difference between survival and death for herself and her children.

For men evaluating partners, non-physical traits of attraction tend to include qualities such as empathy, nurturing, and emotional stability—traits that signal a partner's capacity to build and maintain a harmonious, supportive environment. Again, in a modern context, some of these metrics of attraction can be labeled as "shallow" or "outdated," but these too have existed and been refined over countless years by the Will to Power. These qualities are often viewed as indicators of a mate's ability to successfully raise and care for offspring while contributing to a stable and enduring relationship. Historically, these traits aligned with survival, as a nurturing and cooperative partner greatly increased the likelihood of offspring thriving in challenging environments where success of the family often depended on cohesion and mutual support.

While these traits and preferences may have their roots in early humanity, we now live in the 21st century—a world far removed from the days of hunting for food or migrating with the seasons to survive. This stark shift in lifestyle introduces compelling challenges for romance among humans, as the preferences and instincts shaped by our evolutionary past now intersect with a vastly different social and technological landscape.

We now exist in an age where a living generation of humans has witnessed and experienced the rise of the current technological revolution. From radio and television to the internet and smartphones; technology has come a very long way in a very short period of time. This rapid progression of technology, driven relentlessly by the Will to Power, far outpaces the slower, incremental processes of the same force moving through human evolution.

What happens to human romance and attraction, refined by the Will to Power over millennia, when technology arrives and radically transforms the romantic and dating landscape? The answer lies in the tension between deeply ingrained evolutionary traits and the unprecedented possibilities technology introduces.

For thousands of years, the Will to Power shaped human attraction and mate pairing through face-to-face interactions, physical presence, and environmental cues. Technology, however, has rewritten the rules. Dating apps, social media, and digital communication have created a new arena where both men and women are struggling to adapt.

For women, the rise of social media and dating apps has significantly expanded their potential dating pool, extending beyond men in their local city or town to include options across the country and even the world. While this abundance of choice may seem like an advantage, it can often be overwhelming, making the search for a meaningful connection among endless possibilities seem almost impossible.

For men, these same technologies have dramatically increased competition for attention. No longer are they competing solely with other men in their hunting tribe or immediate community; they now face rivals from across the globe, each vying for the same pool of attention and connection.

Additionally, in the modern age, women no longer need to rely on men for financial or physical support as they once did throughout history. Similarly, men are no longer required to hunt, protect, or provide for their partners in the traditional ways that historically defined their roles. Yet the Will to Power remains unyielding in its movement and continued expression. As a result, both men and women now find themselves scrambling to redefine their roles in romantic partnerships, all while contending with the enduring influence of hundreds of thousands of years of evolutionary refinement in mate selection, physical attraction, and relationship dynamics.

The Will to Power's relentless movement through this new dating landscape has contributed to what many now call "the loneliness epidemic," where both men and women increasingly struggle to find, establish, and maintain meaningful romantic connections. This epidemic is neither the result nor fault of any particular gender, despite claims to the contrary. Rather, it is a consequence of the Will to Power—the force that shaped the very essence of human romance and intimacy—continuing to move through this technological age while human evolution struggles to keep pace. Understanding this dynamic can help one navigate this new social landscape as humanity continues to adapt to a world where romantic courtship and partnership are being redefined on every level.

For those engaged in romantic relationships, the same manifestations of the Will to Power that we've explored in other dynamics are clearly evident. Just as in friendships and group interactions, nearly every romantic relationship sees the natural emergence of dominant and submissive roles. This emergent power dynamic in romantic relationships is universally understood by humans, even if they are not consciously aware of it or unwilling to acknowledge it.

Evidence of this understanding can be found in television and film, where it has long been adopted as a recurring trope in relationships. In the 1950s and 60s, the dominant, dashing husband who led the household, and the submissive, beautiful housewife were the standard archetypes. In more modern productions, the roles have often reversed, portraying the bumbling, overweight husband alongside a beautiful, steadfast wife who holds the household together with her wit and maturity. *The Simpsons* and *Family Guy* serve as quintessential examples of the latter type of this trope.

While these depictions may be exaggerated for the sake of entertainment, they hint at the underlying manifestation and movement of the Will to Power through romantic partnership. Just as in other dynamics, the roles within a romantic relationship are not static. They are continually challenged and refined through the give-and-take between partners that ultimately shapes and refines the relationship as its own entity. Going from the dominant male figure of the 1950's to the more dominant and assertive housewife of modern portrayals helps illustrate how these roles are challenged and changed over time. However, these power dynamics rarely play out as picturesquely as they do in these portrayals.

In some instances, the submissive partner concedes too much in the way of personal growth, relying solely on the relationship itself to serve as the primary avenue of expression for the Will to Power. This is why some may feel they "lose themselves" or "forget who they are" when in longstanding relationships. As the submissive continually acquiesces to the influence of the dominant partner, the Will to Power does not stop moving within the individual. It continues on, refining and amplifying these habits of submission, and can potentially manifest as co-dependence.

Conversely, the dominant partner's behaviors and habits are also further refined. As each subtle power struggle is won, the demands and influence of the dominant partner may grow accordingly and potentially manifest as controlling or abusive behavior toward their partner.

In cases where the power imbalance becomes too great, the Will to Power often manifests as resentment, hostility, emotional withdrawal, and even infidelity. In the case of the submissive, these feelings and behaviors represent the expression of the Will to Power striving toward self-expression and overcoming in defiance of subjugation. In the dominant, they represent the expression of the Will to Power seeking the adversity and challenge that is required for continued growth. Once these feelings take root, they too are refined and optimized by the Will to Power—and usually signal the end of the relationship itself.

However, not all relationships are destined to follow this exact trajectory when dominant and submissive roles are amplified and refined over time. Variations can arise due to the Will to Power's expression in and refinement of individual preference—just as it does in the case of physical attraction. In some relationships, these roles of dominance and submission are explicitly defined between partners, allowing the dynamic to exist in a complementary way. For example, a relationship in which the submissive benefits from the assertiveness of the dominant, while the dominant benefits from the support and temperance of the submissive.

Successful couples seem to intuitively understand this interplay within their relationship even if they aren't consciously aware of it or the Will to Power. Both partners continue to strive for personal expression and growth while serving as both a source of support and challenge for the other. In this instance, the relationship serves as an avenue of perpetual rediscovery and expression of refined individual desires.

While the dominant and submissive roles are still present, the successful couple intuitively understands that these roles are interchangeable throughout the life of a relationship. At times, the submissive will seek to assert their dominance within the relationship, reaffirming their individuality and personal agency. Likewise, at times, the dominant will seek submission within the relationship as an outlet to express vulnerability or subservience. This constant challenging of roles between partners is the Will to Power in action—an endless cycle of assertion, compromise, and personal expression. Understanding and embracing these changing dynamics ensures that the power struggle manifested by the Will to Power remains balanced and that the relationship is refined and optimized toward mutual growth and aligned goals.

In this instance, the Asymptrex being strived for by the Will to Power is one in which the bond between partners has become so optimized and refined that the fluidity between roles has become habits of understanding and reciprocity—such that the terms "dominant" and "submissive" no longer suffice as descriptors of the relationship dynamic.

However, we know the Asymptrex can never be reached. While your initial thought may be something like, "Then my relationship will never be perfect!", it's important to remember that while the Asymptrex is the endpoint that is sought by the Will to Power, it is the journey of striving and optimization that defines its existence and that of life itself. In the case of romantic relationships, this is a disguised blessing, as it reminds us that no matter how good a relationship may be, it can still get even better!

Further Thoughts

It should be explicitly noted that I have used the terms "man" and "woman" within this portion of the book for the sake of simplicity. The observations made of the Will to Power are universal and apply to all genders and sexual orientations. In fact, it is because of the Will to Power's continued influence and refinement of humanity that a wide range of sexual preferences and orientations exist in the first place. The diversity found within humanity serves as proof of the universal and all-inclusive expression of the Will to Power as it forever refines humanity toward its perfected state.

Additionally, the terms "dominant" and "submissive" hold no inherent gender bias or emotional connotations. If you read this portion of the book and consciously or unconsciously assigned gender to these terms, or viewed either as inherently positive or negative, it should serve as evidence of how societal and cultural biases can influence and refine our perception. It is only in acknowledging and removing these shackles from within our minds that we can gain a deeper understanding of not only ourselves but of each other.

To further illustrate that these dominant and submissive manifestations are not inherently negative, I ask you to look no further than the relationship you have with your pets.

Interspecies Relationships: Humans and Pets

With the Will to Power moving through and refining each individual human uniquely, the relationships that form between them remain infinitely complex and ever-changing. However, it is in the predictable behavior of the Will to Power that we are able to find commonalities between all its infinite manifestations. The observations made in regard to the Will to Power moving through human relationships apply to other interactions as well.

Consider the relationship between humans and their pets, particularly cats and dogs. While humans may see themselves as the dominant species on the planet—technologically advanced and capable of shaping the environment to their will—it's worth asking: who really runs your household? Is it you, the human, or is it your fluffy companion who dictates when you wake, where you sit, and how you spend your money? This dynamic illustrates the Will to Power in action, not through conquest or brute force but through adaptation, refinement, and influence.

From the moment a pet enters your home, the Will to Power begins to move through both you and your new companion in direct response to this new relationship. The pet, whether it's a wide-eyed kitten or a wagging puppy, quickly learns to read your behavior, refining its actions to elicit desired outcomes. A meow at the door or a nudge of the food bowl becomes a tool of influence. Over time, these small actions refine your routines: you wake earlier than you'd like to feed them, rearrange your furniture to accommodate them, and budget for toys, vet visits, and special treats. The pet refines its ability to control and exert influence over its environment, and you adapt in response.

This isn't dominance in the traditional sense; it's a manifestation of the Will to Power as a neutral force. The cat doesn't dominate you out of a desire to subjugate, nor do you submit out of weakness. Instead, the interplay of your desires and theirs creates a dynamic in which the force moves through both parties, constantly shaping and refining the relationship—just as it does in all other forms of relationships.

The pet learns your rhythms and preferences, becoming more adept at using its behaviors to influence your actions. Meanwhile, you refine your own behaviors in response—feeding them at the right time, ensuring their needs are met, and even going out of your way to make them happy. This process creates a symbiotic relationship where both parties display dominance and submission, yet, as your cat wakes you at 4 a.m. for the fourth time this week, it can often feel as though the pet is the one calling the shots.

The humor of realizing that your cat may "own" you offers a deeper lesson in the adaptability of the Will to Power. It's not about who is "stronger" or more capable; it's about who can adapt, refine, and assert influence most effectively. Your cat may not be the apex predator of the planet, but it has found a way to domesticate the species that is—proving that dominance is as much about subtlety and connection as it is about raw power.

By examining the relationships we cultivate with our pets, we're able to clearly see the Will to Power in action without the societal or cultural influences that may hinder our ability to analyze this force in the context of other human relationship dynamics. In this case, we clearly see the Will to Power move through both pet and owner, driving mutual adaptation and influencing every aspect of the relationship toward a bond of companionship and mutual understanding. The same force that shapes the rise and fall of civilizations also dictates why you find yourself buying gourmet treats for a cat who sleeps on your laptop. The Will to Power, as always, remains neutral, refining and reshaping everything it touches toward perfection—even your pets.

Conclusion

In this chapter, we have delved deeply into the manifestation of the Will to Power in humans, uncovering its role as a neutral, relentless force shaping every aspect of human thought, behavior, and relationships. Its impartial nature and boundless adaptability make it a driver of both triumph and turmoil, depending on how it is allowed to manifest.

We began by emphasizing that "good" and "bad" do not apply to the Will to Power. This neutrality underscores its ability to lead individuals toward either mastery or destruction, with outcomes determined by the channels through which this force flows. Whether fostering a life of discipline and achievement or refining destructive habits, the Will to Power remains indifferent, seeking only to move toward the Asymptrex.

Through the exploration of habits, we saw how they serve as reflections of the Will to Power's influence. Habits are the tangible results of the force's optimization, shaping our lives with unrelenting efficiency—with or without our conscious consent. Muscle memory and daily routines exemplify its streamlining power, while human self-awareness and intent grant us the invaluable ability to shape these habits consciously, redirecting the Will to Power toward outcomes we desire.

The section "8 Billion Minds and Counting" demonstrated the unique pathways through which the Will to Power manifests in every individual. The example of the speedrunning community revealed how this force drives mastery and innovation, even in the most niche pursuits. Yet, this same relentless drive also highlights the dual nature of the Will to Power, capable of inspiring greatness or enabling destruction.

We further explored the darker side of this force in "If it can be cheated, it will be cheated." Here, the Will to Power's drive for dominance and perfection was shown to override ethical considerations, manifesting in dishonesty and manipulation. From gaming to corporate scandals, this section revealed how the Will to Power exploits every available avenue, challenging us to design systems that minimize opportunities for its destructive expressions.

Moving to interpersonal relationships, we saw how the Will to Power shapes the dynamics between individuals and groups, driving the interplay of dominance and submission. In parent-child relationships, this force refines the balance between guidance and independence. In friendships, it fosters mutual growth or destructive co dependence. In group dynamics, it revealed the natural emergence of hierarchies and social structures, and the individual drive between cooperation and self-assertion that defines one's relationship to the larger community.

In large collectives, we explored how the Will to Power manifests as the driving force behind the formation and evolution of societal structures, governance, and cultural movements. This force drives the pursuit of progress and innovation, while also exposing vulnerabilities that manifest as conflict, corruption, and exploitation. By recognizing its movement within these vast collectives, we see how the same force that shapes individual and small-group interactions also defines the trajectory of entire civilizations, urging us to consciously channel its energy toward collective growth and harmony rather than division and imbalance.

The examination of romantic relationships revealed the intricate ways the Will to Power has shaped attraction, mate selection, and the ever-evolving roles of romantic partners. It drives the dynamic interplay between dominance and submission, shaping the balance of power that defines the partnership. As relationships progress, this force refines the emotional connection between individuals, fostering opportunities for growth, self-discovery, and mutual understanding. However, if left to manifest unchecked, we see how the Will to Power can refine a romantic relationship toward imbalance and negative behaviors that ultimately lead to its demise.

Lastly, in interspecies relationships, we saw how the Will to Power transcends humanity, shaping the bonds we share with our pets. These relationships exemplify the subtle interplay of influence, adaptation, and mutual refinement, providing a pure example of the force's movement through relationships without societal or cultural interference.

Throughout this chapter, the Will to Power has been revealed as a constant, driving force that refines, optimizes, and transforms all aspects of human existence. By understanding how it manifests in our habits, thoughts, and relationships, we gain the ability to guide its flow consciously. In doing so, we can embrace the Will to Power as the fundamental force it is and use our understanding of it to cultivate lives of purpose, resilience, and growth.

How to use the Will to Power

Now that you've started recognizing the Will to Power as it moves through all of existence, it's time to explore how this understanding can empower you to shape your life, guide its direction, and influence the world around you.

Change & Habit Formation

So, you understand the Will to Power and recognize it in the world around you, yet you struggle to see how it moves through you personally. You feel directionless—unsure of your path. What should you do?

First, remember that the Will to Power is always moving through you, whether you recognize it or not. It is indifferent to your choices, neither favoring success nor failure. It will refine whatever habits you allow to manifest, simply taking you along for the ride—if you let it. That's why deep and honest self-reflection is crucial. Only by defining what you truly want can you begin to guide the Will to Power toward the life you desire.

Since the Will to Power is always moving through you like a powerful river, it's imperative that you be the captain of the ship riding upon that river. You can exert force over the Will to Power by guiding its flow in a direction that serves your goals, desires, and purpose. The best way to do this is to define the ways in which you allow it to move through your life via your habits and lifestyle. By consciously shaping your thoughts and actions, you can influence the Will to Power, ensuring it refines and optimizes your life in alignment with your aspirations.

For example, let's say one of your life goals is to reach a certain level of health and fitness, but you are currently an overweight alcoholic. How do you manipulate and use your understanding of the Will to Power to achieve your goal?

The first thing you should do is limit the ways in which the Will to Power can move. It's pretty tough to be an alcoholic if there is no way for you to get your hands on any alcohol. If you were suddenly stranded on a deserted island with no hope of rescue, you would have no choice but to give up drinking—and the Will to Power would flow through you accordingly.

It would be quite difficult and uncomfortable at first, but because the Will to Power is limited by your environment, it has no choice but to flow through you in such a way that you become better and better able to deal with not having alcohol—until eventually, your desire for it all but fades away.

The same would apply to replacing your deep-dish pizza eating habits with a diet of healthier foods. If you're stuck on that island, you're not going to be able to easily consume five-thousand calories of garbage food every day. You'll quickly become grateful for the fruits and vegetables you're able to forage and, courtesy of the Will to Power, continuously get better at finding and procuring.

While that is a very basic, crude, brute-force example, it perfectly illustrates how people can manipulate the way in which the Will to Power moves through their lives by controlling their environment. It's going to move through your life no matter what, so it's up to you to do your best to set the rules and boundaries in which it can manifest and operate.

But what if you don't know what you want to do with your life yet? What if you just haven't figured it out? Don't worry, there's still plenty you can do!

I would start by making it my goal to find my goal—to figure out what would make me happy and give me a feeling of purpose in life. To that end, I would begin to live my life in such a way that it allows the Will to Power to move through me with great ease. I would attempt to become the best vessel I could for the Will to Power—to live in harmony with it. This means eating healthily, exercising, loving myself and others, and generally just living a lifestyle that keeps both my mind and body prepared for whatever the Will to Power may have in store for me.

Finally, I would actively seek out new experiences until I discovered a cause that truly stirred my soul. Once I found it, I would reshape my environment to ensure the Will to Power had no choice but to refine and optimize my life toward that new direction.

"How do I know when I've found it?"

Since every mind is different, I can't answer this question for you. I can only tell you what has worked for me. If you look forward to it—if it's the first thing you think about when you wake up and the last thing on your mind when you go to bed, then it is worth pursuing.

Adversity is Required

It's important to remember that the Will to Power does not exist without adversity. After all, it is a force that seeks to optimize and refine all things to their perfect state. Without adversity there is no need for refinement nor optimization.

In all cases, the adversity required for the Will to Power's continued movement comes in the form of the force interacting with another iteration of itself. The predator-prey dynamic from the chapter on nature is an excellent example of this.

When one is trying to cultivate productive habits, behaviors, and patterns of thought, adversity is also always present. In this case, the Will to Power manifests as its inverse in the form of self-doubt, negative self-talk, and procrastination. I refer to this manifestation as Inner-Adversity.

Take, for example, the unfolded clean clothes that have been sitting in the basket for over a week. You consciously know you need to fold them and that doing so would only require 15-20 minutes of your time, yet there they continue to sit. The thought of needing to fold your clothes continuously pops up within your mind throughout the week, hanging over your head like a dark, little cloud. However, the manifestation of Inner-Adversity continues to win each small battle. You continually tell yourself, "I'll get them in the morning" or "I'll do it tomorrow", until eventually, you've steadily picked out and worn so many pieces of clothing from the basket that it's time to do laundry again, and the battle of folding your clothes begins anew. Yes, the Will to Power is even the reason for your unfolded laundry!

While this is a lighthearted and humorous example, it perfectly illustrates the manifestation of Inner-Adversity. It's this inverse manifestation of the Will to Power within our own thoughts that creates the adversity required for the force's continued movement and our own internal growth. It explains why cultivating new patterns of thoughts and habits can be difficult.

For example, consider the intent to start a new lifestyle habit of going to the gym. At first, it may be incredibly awkward. You're in a new place, surrounded by people you don't know, many of whom appear further along in their fitness journey than you—and you barely understand what much of the equipment is for, much less how to use it. You walk for a while on the treadmill and eventually leave.

You said you were going to go daily. However, once the time arrives to go the next day, you're flooded with self-sabotaging thoughts and feelings— *"I don't even know what to do there. Everyone else looks at me. I just feel so out of place."* Eventually, you end up saying, "I'll just go tomorrow," but tomorrow never comes and Inner-Adversity wins the battle. This is the story for millions of people who've attempted such a transformation. However, for those that understand the Will to Power, the story can play out quite differently.

As we've previously discussed, the Will to Power likes habits and forms them as a matter of fact. This is why you reach a point in your creation of habits where the manifestation of Inner-Adversity becomes less and less prominent over time. It's in recognizing the Will to Power as both the drive that desires to create change, and the inverse manifestation of self-doubt that attempts to challenge that change, where the greatest strength of understanding this force lies.

In the case of this example, because you recognize and can identify these self-sabotaging thoughts as a manifestation of the Will to Power, you are more able to confront and dismiss them. Instead of skipping the gym the following day, you get in your car and go—despite your mind telling you the whole way, "Hey, let's just get some fast food and go home. It's easier!" Fast forward a couple weeks of repeated visits, and the internal battle of the Will to Power over going to the gym has been replaced by the initial formation of habit. Now, not only does this Inner-Adversity seem to manifest less and less, but you actually begin to look forward to going to the gym as routinely as you can.

There is great power in knowing that your continued action will *always* be rewarded by the Will to Power through the formation of new patterns of thought and habits. It's this unequivocal assurance that the Will to Power provides that can help you begin seemingly impossible journeys and transformations.

However, while Inner-Adversity will manifest less and less as habit formation solidifies, it never fully dissipates. For without this conflict, the Will to Power cannot exist. This truth is evident even in examples of self-destruction.

Take, for example, when one is cultivating destructive habits like alcoholism and substance abuse. Inner-Adversity is still present in the form of thoughts and desires that seek to break those habits; "*I know this is bad for me. I should stop doing this. I wish I were different.*" Even if one has accepted these habits as unchangeable and simply a part of one's life, Inner-Adversity will still forever manifest. This means that even if you were purposely trying to sabotage your life—even as the Will to Power makes you more proficient at that sabotage—you would still meet resistance!

It's this dual understanding of the Will to Power and how it manifests within our own thoughts and habits that not only helps us understand why we struggle but also gives us the confidence and courage to embrace that struggle as a necessary part of growth—better equipping us to meet it head-on and overcome it.

Perhaps it is in this constant, moment-to-moment struggle between the Will to Power and Inner-Adversity that we glimpse the true nature of our greatest asset: free will.

A Few Thoughts on Free Will

For centuries, Free Will has been debated—framed as either an absolute human freedom or an illusion dictated by determinism. But both views are incomplete. Free Will is neither a constant state nor an illusion—it is an inherent quality of all beings capable of conscious choice, expressed as a mechanism that occurs at the peak of refinement between the Will to Power and its inverse, Inner-Adversity.

Some of our decisions may be made unconsciously or instinctively as a product of our own refinement—similar to muscle memory. However, we still exhibit Free Will through conscious choice.

Do I fold my laundry or do I not?
Will I have another drink or will I not?
Do I call in sick to work or do I not?

Each of these outcomes exists in the Unseen as potential. The Will to Power is refining both possibilities toward existence, but only one can manifest. Free Will is the decisive moment of choice that determines which path continues into reality—where it will continue refining toward the Asymptrex—and which path is erased.

Free Will is not just personal agency; it is the very force that determines what gets to exist. Every act of choice is an act of creation and destruction, selecting one version of reality while erasing all others. In exercising Free Will, you become the architect of your own reality by choosing which outcome manifests as existence and continues on.

Free Will is not an anomaly or a mystery. It is the core process that bridges the Will to Power's movement between the Unseen and existence. Free Will is, without question, our most awesome ability.

Analysis & Prediction

One of the most valuable things about understanding the Will to Power is that it can be used to find order in seemingly chaotic and random occurrences. Since the Will to Power moves through and influences everything without exception, being able to view things through a lens of this force allows one to find a point of commonality from which a more comprehensive analysis can be conducted.

Prediction and understanding are far and away the most valuable insights I've gained from understanding the Will to Power. Events and occurrences that seem impossible to decode can become quite simple to understand when viewed through a lens of this force.

To illustrate this, I offer an example from my own life. I will preface this story by saying that it is in no way intended to be financial advice and shouldn't be taken as such.

The Will to Power through Currency

I first learned about Bitcoin when a single coin was worth less than $20 USD. While I didn't delve deeply into the underlying technology, I was fascinated by its potential and kept a loose eye on its progress and adoption around the world. Unfortunately, I was rarely in a secure enough financial position to invest, and the few times I did left me riddled with anxiety because I was unable to predict its short- or long-term trajectory. That all changed when I began to study and understand the Will to Power.

Once I began to view Bitcoin through a lens of the Will to Power, it began to make perfect sense that digital currency was absolutely going to be a part of the future. After all, using hard currency—paper money and coins—was eventually going to become too inefficient for the Will to Power's liking. It would only be a matter of time before Bitcoin and digital currency do to hard currency what email and text messaging did to traditional mail. By understanding the Will to Power, it became apparent to me that it wasn't a question of "if" this would happen, but "when."

Fast forward a few years, and it's 2022. Bitcoin has begun to crash from its peak of around $70,000. While watching the price continue to fall month after month, I knew that this crash would be the last great buying opportunity of my lifetime. However, as usual, I didn't have an income that provided me with a surplus of cash to invest. I needed my money for day-to-day and month-to-month expenses that would ensure

I survived and that my bills were getting paid. However, even if I wasn't in a position to take advantage of what I saw coming, there were those in my family who were. I couldn't let my knowledge go to waste.

I began talking with my sister about Bitcoin and the great buying opportunity I saw on the horizon. Like most people, she had heard of Bitcoin before, but only through occasional headlines and discussions with coworkers which would pop up when Bitcoin was trending upwards. She really didn't know much about it or the technology behind it, but she knew I had been following it for years.

After a crash course in Bitcoin 101 and some convincing, she decided she was ready to pull the trigger using a significant portion of her savings. I won't disclose the exact amount, but it was enough to make me realize the enormous amount of trust she was placing in me and my analysis.

I didn't tell her that my confidence in her investment came from my understanding of the Will to Power—I figured that might make me sound a bit crazy. But the truth is, it was the only reason I felt comfortable advising her to go forward.

After all, investing my own money and losing it would have been one thing; I'd only be harming myself. But advising her to invest and potentially lose a substantial portion of her savings was a completely different story. If I were wrong, it could severely harm her family and possibly do irreparable damage to our relationship.

The weight of that responsibility was almost too much to bear. But my understanding of the Will to Power, combined with my cumulative knowledge of Bitcoin and digital currency, gave me the confidence to believe this wouldn't end in disaster. Instead, I was convinced it would help set her and her family up for a much brighter future.

Over the next couple of months, I helped her get investment accounts set up in preparation for the impending crash. Then it came. As Bitcoin began plunging from $30,000 to $18,000, I told her it was time. I coached her through making several buys during this downturn until the entirety of her investment capital was spent. While the media and investing public were touting the end of Bitcoin and selling, she was buying.

Much to my dismay, the price continued to drop over the next couple of months. I won't lie—at this point, I started to get a little nervous, even as I reassured my sister. "As long as you can leave your money there and hold for a couple of years, the price will recover," I told her. "It's best to set it and forget it. Checking the price every day will only drive you crazy."

Fortunately, she was in a position where she could afford to leave the investment untouched without straining her family's day-to-day lifestyle—and she did exactly that.

Nearly three years later, her initial investment has grown to more than five times its original value—and it's still climbing. I had successfully used my understanding of the Will to Power to capitalize on the world around me. Without that knowledge, I would have never advised her to make such a significant investment. There's no amount of money that would justify risking my relationship with her and her family—it's far too precious to me.

But in my mind, the risk wasn't as great as it seemed. I wasn't just betting on Bitcoin, the technology behind it, or the knowledge I had accumulated about it over the years. I was betting on my understanding of the Will to Power—and it behaved exactly as I anticipated. That bet paid off. This outcome wasn't just a matter of luck or market speculation. It was the result of recognizing the patterns shaped by the Will to Power and aligning with its direction.

While Bitcoin itself remains subject to market fluctuations and human behavior, its rise mirrors the broader trajectory of progress driven by the Will to Power—a force that constantly seeks to refine and optimize systems, making traditional currencies increasingly inefficient by comparison.

This is just one example of how your understanding of the Will to Power can be used to shape your life and influence the world around you. By grasping how this force behaves, you can uncover patterns and find predictability in what might seem like chaos.

Further Clarity

Aside from predicting the likely progression of emergent technologies, this same understanding can be applied to other areas as well. Perhaps you're struggling to understand the behavior of a friend, relative, or coworker. By analyzing their behavior through a lens of the Will to Power, you may be able to determine how the force is driving their beliefs and actions.

Because you understand the Will to Power, you will begin to view all your relationships in a profoundly different way. You won't view them solely in terms of the power dynamics that were used to explain the concept previously. You will see beyond them, focusing primarily on how the Will to Power is manifesting as a whole in the behavior of your child, your sister, your boss, and so on. You will see how the Will to Power manifests as individual ambition and self-assertion; you will see the habits they've allowed the Will to Power to refine; and you will see them win and lose battles with Inner-Adversity. You will no longer just hear and see them; you will begin to *understand* them. This is especially true when interacting with those who aren't viewing the world and existence through the same lens as you are now.

Additionally, this same logic can be applied to analyzing the world at large, helping one gain a better understanding of social and political climates that may seem unclear. However, it should be noted that analyzing the world in this fashion can lead to some uncomfortable realizations—such as understanding that certain political movements may not serve the best interests of the people, but instead prioritize the personal enrichment, financially or otherwise, of the politicians behind them—despite what they may say. To view and analyze the world through a lens of the Will to Power is to see it as it truly is—raw and unfiltered, with both its beauty and brutality on full display.

Implications of the Will to Power

The Will to Power is undeniable. We see it move through everything in existence. But what does this mean for the future? With an understanding of this force, we can begin to analyze and even anticipate the trajectory of nearly any aspect of life with a greater degree of certainty.

The Future of Humanity

When looking at humanity through a lens of the Will to Power, one thing becomes quite clear. Humans will continue to find ways to prolong their lives. If you look at medical advancements throughout human history, it's extremely easy to see how the Will to Power has moved through this area of study and practice. Illnesses and injuries that were death sentences only fifty years ago are now manageable or even curable.

Diseases that currently plague modern humanity, like cancer, are not only likely, but nearly guaranteed to be solved. How this will be done is a question open to much debate and speculation. Will we figure out a way to expel the disease from the body through some form of genetic manipulation? Will we develop nanotechnology that sees humans using microscopic robots to eliminate the disease from within the body? Who knows? But the one thing we can say for certain is that this medical milestone *will* be achieved—it's simply a matter of time.

The merging of human and machine is something that is already beginning to happen. You can see it today in modern medicine where people are using artificial implants to address medical issues. Things like artificial hearts, lungs, and limbs, for example. As I write this, I am scheduled for cataract surgery where the organic lens in my eye will be replaced with an artificial one. As the Will to Power continues to move, it seems inevitable that there will continue to be a deeper merging of human and machine.

A good example of this merging of human and machine is evident every time you go out in public and see countless people on their smartphones. While this isn't a merging in the biological sense, it is a form of merging, nonetheless. We've entered an age and time where the average human essentially has a computer with the sum of the world's knowledge in their hand. How long will it be before carrying around this device becomes too clunky and inefficient?

Viewing this scenario through a lens of the Will to Power, it seems only natural that doing away with the device entirely and simply using our mind would be a logical path for the Will to Power to take. In fact, there are already people and companies out there that are attempting to do just this. For example, Elon Musk's Neuralink project is an attempt to link the human brain directly to computers and devices by developing a brain-computer interface. Such an idea seemed like outlandish science fiction only ten years ago, and yet, here we are watching human trials get underway.

A Future with Artificial Intelligence

Watching the Will to Power move through the field of artificial intelligence (AI) has been as fascinating as it is terrifying. Its mainstream adoption started as a few simple learning models that could teach themselves how to master video games and, rather quickly, became the new arms race of the 21st century.

Humans are watching in real time as the Will to Power races through this new entity and are witnessing the huge leaps in progress in regard to both functionality and usability. Even though the technology is still in its infancy, we're already starting to feel the effects of lost jobs and wages due to AI systems being able to match and even exceed experts in various fields like writing, graphic design, coding, marketing, and so many more.

Because we understand the Will to Power, we can attempt to get an idea of what the future might look like in a world where AI is better than humans at doing a vast majority of tasks.

The first and most pressing concern regarding the inevitable adoption of AI is lost jobs and wages. As the Will to Power races through a capitalist society, companies are forever looking for ways to cut costs and maximize profits—even at the expense of both their customers and employees. What better way to achieve this than to replace your human labor—labor that needs to eat, sleep, be paid, and still makes mistakes—with AI labor? It's already happening, quietly, behind the scenes.

As of this writing, we're seeing layoffs in a wide range of industries, particularly the tech industry, continuing to grow month over month while college students with 4.0 GPAs from prestigious schools are struggling to find employment because companies are instituting hiring freezes due to AI adoption. Why hire a person to write code for your company at a cost of $150K+ per year when you can hire an AI agent that will not only do the job better, but also requires no days off, no sleep, no vacations, and is a fraction of the cost of its human counterpart? This is the chilling reality of the Will to Power moving simultaneously through capitalism and AI; and I fear it's only going to get worse.

If our global response to Covid-19 serves as any indication, humanity is simply not equipped to deal with the looming crisis that AI and robotics will unleash upon society. Perhaps if we were proactive, we could avert disaster, but because AI is already being adopted by corporations and governments across the world, by the time people realize there is a problem, it will already be too late.

It reminds me of living through the golden age and mass adoption years of the internet. It started as a niche hobby for nerds like me in the late 1990s. It was little more than gaming and chatrooms back then, but fast forward only ten years later and the internet is in the palm of nearly every first-world citizen on the planet courtesy of smartphones. The internet went from niche technology to permeating all of modern society, and it happened so swiftly and quietly that nobody seemed to notice. Now, you can barely function in modern society without internet access. I see AI's current state and trajectory mirroring the adoption of the internet. It will quickly and quietly permeate every facet of human society before humanity even realizes what has happened.

The first major problem to arise from this scenario will come in the form of job losses. AI is already replacing people in a wide array of jobs such as writers, customer service reps, graphic designers, data analysts, financial analysts, data entry, coders, personal assistants, video game designers, therapists, and the list goes on—and on. These job losses bring us to the second major problem that humanity will face in an AI-driven future: wealth inequality.

As millions of people are steadily replaced by AI in the workforce, in the background, a tipping point will be reached, and the financial fallout will be both swift and devastating. This will cause the current wealth inequality problems plaguing the world to grow exponentially. While companies and governments battle it out in a never-ending race to create and control the most powerful AI systems in the world, it's the common citizen that will be left behind. Seemingly out of nowhere, the average person may find themselves living in a world they can no longer financially afford to be a part of.

If the scenario I've described is a likely progression path of the Will to Power through AI and capitalism, then it brings us to an obvious question: "How will the Will to Power continue to move through humanity in light of these new challenges?" Let's explore this question by continuing with our analysis to see the likely paths the Will to Power might take.

Universal Basic Income

The first and most likely outcome of living in such a world is universal basic income (UBI). If millions upon millions of people are suddenly (in the scope of human society, 10-20 years is rather sudden) without work and unable to compete with AI agents and robots that are continuously making up more and more of the world's workforce, it seems almost certain that some form of UBI will be implemented.

While free money sounds good on paper, it is hardly a complete solution—especially in a capitalist society. It is more of a stop-gap measure that will come with its own set of problems. If history is any indication, the amount of the stipend is likely to be at or below poverty level—meaning, it will barely be enough for people to survive on, let alone thrive on. You will have millions of people on a fixed income with little or no hope of ever advancing beyond this financial class. Humans will seek out ways to improve their mobility financially and societally—as we know, the Will to Power guarantees this. This leads us to another possible progression path that may be taken in attempting to transition to an AI-driven future: transhumanism.

Transhumanism

If UBI is not enough to ensure that the majority of humans are able to lead meaningful and fulfilling lives, transhumanism—the use of technology to enhance human ability—could be the next likely progression path of the Will to Power.

For those who can afford it, transhumanism may be a way to narrow the gap between humans and AI. Even very advanced AI is likely to still have flaws in reasoning that humans simply will not have. For example, while AI excels in processing data and identifying patterns, it often struggles with contextual understanding, moral judgment, and adaptability to novel or ambiguous situations. Because of this, it could be advantageous for humanity to enhance itself via technology such that human decision making and intuition is accentuated by the precision and speed of AI. The superintelligence that AI companies and enthusiasts are striving to achieve may only be possible through transhumanism—where the best qualities of both entities produce something entirely new.

However, this will also come with its own set of problems. Problems like inequality will be amplified when a large portion of the population, specifically those whose sole income is UBI, cannot afford augmentation to keep up with their wealthier counterparts. For example, wealthier individuals could gain access to cognitive or physical enhancements that grant them outsized advantages in productivity, lifespan, or influence, further consolidating power and leaving UBI-dependent individuals behind in a new caste system.

Transhumanism also brings into question human identity and what it means to be human. How much augmentation is permissible—how advanced can abilities become—before one is no longer considered human? If physical and cognitive augmentations can replace or surpass natural abilities, where do we draw the line between human and machine? Does identity remain tied to biology, or will it evolve alongside technology?

Additionally, there are issues of prejudice to consider. Given humanity's history of conflict over perceived differences, such as race, religion, and socioeconomic status, the rise of transhuman individuals could ignite new forms of prejudice and division, creating societal rifts that mirror and amplify those of the past. How extreme will the hate and violence become toward transhuman individuals should this practice of augmentation become normalized?

Perhaps transhumanism is the initial catalyst that brings about the emergence of the Übermensch that Nietzsche describes in his philosophy—a being who transcends traditional human limitations and redefines what it means to live with purpose and mastery in an AI-dominated world. But I digress.

Global Societal Reform

Whether UBI or transhumanism succeed or fail in softening the blow of mass AI and robotics adoption, one outcome seems inevitable: societal reform. The disruptive power of these technologies will compel governments worldwide to implement new regulations and laws governing their use and production.

While the precise form of these regulations is difficult to predict, key questions must be addressed. Will ethics committees be formed to guide and govern AI adoption and use? Will regulatory measures be introduced to pace the transition, mitigating the risk of societal upheaval? Could certain applications of AI and robotics be outlawed in specific industries? These are but a few possible ways world governments could be proactive in helping to shape the way in which this technology is integrated into humanity.

Additionally, I believe it is only by understanding the Will to Power and recognizing how AI embodies this force so transparently that humanity can design safeguards capable of balancing progress with societal stability. Leaders must not ignore the potential consequences of this technological revolution. If they attempt to dismiss these challenges or prioritize short-term gains over the welfare of the average citizen, the Will to Power will be left with but one outlet—causing it to manifest in its most turbulent form: revolution.

A Positive Return to Humanity

While the previous scenario paints a rather bleak outlook for the immediate future, it is in no way set in stone. In fact, it is likely that due to the widespread adoption of the internet, AI, and robotics, we will see the Will to Power manifest in some unexpected and profoundly positive ways.

One such outcome is the resurgence of third spaces—physical environments like bars, arcades, pool halls, dance halls, malls, and community parks that serve as social hubs where people can interact face-to-face.

In a world where humans are more digitally connected than ever yet increasingly isolated, the drive for real-world community and physical interaction will not fade—it will intensify. As AI and automation remove human presence from many aspects of daily life, people will instinctively seek out places where they can experience genuine, unscripted, human-to-human engagement. This revival will not be merely nostalgia; it will be a direct manifestation of the Will to Power as it seeks to meet the drive for authentic human companionship.

Bars and pubs may return as social anchors within communities. No AI-driven chatroom or social media feed can replicate the atmosphere of a lively bar, the energy of a crowded venue, or the warmth of in-person conversation. People will return to these spaces not just for drinks, but for the real, unfiltered human experience that cannot be simulated online.

We may also see a renaissance of arcades and gaming halls. Online competitive gaming and skill-based entertainment is increasingly losing its luster as the improvement and adoption of AI continues. The online gaming landscape holds little appeal when one can no longer tell the difference between a real human opponent and an advanced AI bot. Gamers and hobbyists will crave the authenticity that is only possible in real-world interactions where the physical presence of others creates genuine collaborations, rivalries, and celebrations that no digital medium can ever replicate.

Dance halls and live music venues offer a glimpse into why third spaces won't just persist; they will thrive. Unlike other venues impacted by the digital shift, these spaces have remained largely immune, with live shows and nightclubs maintaining their relevance. However, as we move into the future, their importance and popularity will only continue to grow.

Additionally, we're likely to see renewed interest and investment in community parks and recreational centers. These spaces will expand beyond merely being places to go for a walk and will transform into legitimate communal hubs where friendly interactions with others are not only welcomed but anticipated.

This isn't just wishful thinking—it's a highly probable manifestation of the Will to Power in humans in response to the constraints of an ever-growing technological cage. Look around your local community or city, and you may already see the early signs of this resurgence taking shape. This is more than a return to old traditions; it is the next evolution of human connection in a world that has never needed it more. I invite you to become part of this resurgence and help shape the cultural renaissance that has already begun.

Reflections of the Will to Power

As we near the end of this book, I'd like to use this section to offer some reflections about the content we've discussed and some final words.

The Will to Power: The Undeniable Constant

From the moment you opened this book, the Will to Power has been revealing itself to you—not just as a theory, but as the underlying force that moves through all things.

You have seen how it manifests in nature, how it drives human behavior and relationships, how it shapes technology, competition, progress, and destruction alike. You have seen how it refines, optimizes, and perfects everything it touches—including you.

The Will to Power does not ask for belief, nor does it require recognition. Like gravity, it exists whether you acknowledge it or not—moving through your thoughts, struggles, triumphs, and failures. It is the reason behind all things.

The question is no longer whether the Will to Power is real. The question is: What will you do with this new understanding?

The Journey You've Taken

At the beginning of this book, you may have believed your actions and choices were entirely your own. That remains true. But now, you also recognize that beneath every decision, the Will to Power has always been present—moving through you, shaping your thoughts, refining your habits, and amplifying the direction of your life. Your choices are still yours, but with this understanding, you can now wield them with greater awareness and intention.

You have learned that the Will to Power is not an external force pressing upon you, but a force that flows through and within you. It is what has driven your ambitions, your desires, your moments of resistance, and your greatest acts of perseverance. It is the force that has pushed humanity forward and the force that has torn civilizations apart. It is neither good nor evil—it simply is.

This book has explored the Will to Power through history, technology, human behavior, and beyond. But its reach extends further still—to the films you watch, the music you listen to, even to the art that shapes culture itself. Now that you have seen its motion in one domain, you will begin to recognize it everywhere.

Go ahead and look around; take in the world through your new eyes. Simply look for the Will to Power in anything, and you will find it. The question now is: where will you see it next?

A Final Example: The Will to Power in Action

Before this journey ends, I will show you one final proof of the Will to Power's movement—not through abstract theory or distant examples, but through something real.

The very existence of this book is a case study in the force that has shaped all things. The same principles you have studied in these pages—struggle, refinement, optimization, and overcoming—are the very principles that brought this book into being.

You are about to see the Will to Power in action—embedded in the very thoughts, choices, and actions that brought *The Reason for Everything* from the Unseen and into existence.

If the ideas within this book haven't fully settled yet, this final example may bring them into focus in a profoundly meaningful way.

The Reason for Everything as a Case Study of The Will to Power

Without question, writing and releasing this work is by far one of the most challenging things I've ever attempted in my life. What began as a topic of casual discussion between my brother and me turned into something of an obsession within my mind. I never intended to be a philosopher or writer, and I will be the first to say that I am not qualified to call myself either of those things.

However, over the years, the Will to Power kept showing up in our conversations again and again. We would be discussing something seemingly innocuous and in nearly every instance it would lead back to identifying the Will to Power. At some point, it went from being something interesting to note within our conversations to being the explanation for pretty much everything we discussed.

For years, I kept remarking, "It's so fascinating! I should write about this." I knew of Nietzsche and his work courtesy of the conversations with my brother, but I wanted a book that both explained and viewed the Will to Power as we had come to understand it. Little did I realize that the Will to Power was already at work, refining this very idea within my mind.

One evening, as I sat bemoaning the ongoing struggles of my current employment and income with my brother, the Will to Power popped up again in our conversation, and again I remarked, "I really should write that book." It was in that moment that something changed—a tipping point within my mind was reached, and I realized that I was probably going to go to my grave still repeating that phrase. Given the routine and stagnation of my life, if I hadn't written the book already, it was likely that I never would.

This realization plagued my mind. I spent the next several days contemplating the thought, until I finally imagined myself at the end of my life. As I lay there on my deathbed awaiting the end, would I have any regrets? I pondered the question for a while and realized that in that moment, I would have but one regret: that I never wrote the book

I had talked about for years. It was this one singular regret that broke the bough and set ablaze the Will to Power's movement through me toward the creation of this work.

After discussing it with my brother and father, with whom I lived and shared bills, I immediately quit my job and began restructuring my routine to begin writing. I owe them both a tremendous amount of gratitude for supporting me through the creation of this work. For without them, I would never have been able to drop everything and focus solely on its production—an endeavor that was so much harder than I could have ever anticipated.

I didn't realize it at the time, but that entire sequence of events was a pristine example of the Will to Power in action. It refined my thoughts, my actions, and even the restructuring of my environment and circumstances to influence its flow such that *The Reason for Everything* was now leaving the realm of the Unseen and manifesting as existence through my writing.

The pages came quickly, at first. I was simply writing all the ideas and realizations I had cultivated about the Will to Power over the years. However, the enormity of the subject quickly became overwhelming. The Will to Power permeates all of existence, and minds much greater than my own had already written upon the subject. How in the world do I—neither a writer, scholar, nor philosopher—attempt to explain and expand upon such a concept? Who was I to present such a profound idea to the world?

Thankfully, these overwhelming thoughts didn't halt my progress. After all, my family was making sacrifices to allow me this opportunity to write, and I couldn't squander it. I had no choice but to continue regardless of my doubts and the overwhelming complexity of the topic. It was during this period of writing that I began to notice something interesting. I became increasingly aware of how the very force I sought to explain—the Will to Power—was manifesting itself throughout the process of writing *The Reason for Everything*. The Will to Power was essentially moving through and refining its own explanation! This realization not only reinforced my belief in its universality but also became a case study in how it moves through both creation and dissemination.

The pages continued to grow as did my understanding of the Will to Power. While I may have been a novice in my understanding of the subject at the beginning, I was quickly becoming an expert. It seemed that the more I wrote and the more I discovered, the more there was to write and to discover. I realized that I could spend a hundred lifetimes writing on the subject and still barely scratch the surface of explaining all the ways the Will to Power influences existence.

This realization was yet again the force itself at work. I decided that I was not the person who would write the complete compendium on the Will to Power. I was the one who would write the book that attempts to bring the concept into the modern era—reintroducing it to the collective consciousness of humanity. With a concept as vast and all-encompassing as the Will to Power, attempting to introduce the idea by listing and examining every single possible iteration of the force was not only impossible, but would be counter to the very goal I was hoping to achieve. I made the conscious decision to aim for a shorter, more concise introduction to the topic—and in doing so, I again saw the Will to Power refining and shaping its own expression.

As the book neared completion, my progress slowed significantly. I had read and reread my own thoughts so many times that their impact and importance began to feel less profound. The Will to Power, which had driven me to create this work, was now urging me toward greater challenges, demanding new adversities to refine my understanding of its continued expression beyond the ideas I've shared here. What I had written no longer provided the struggle necessary for continued growth. This was how I knew it was time to conclude *The Reason for Everything* and release it into the world.

However, while publishing this work marks the end of the Will to Power's movement through its creation, its influence remains within the work itself. Once released, the book becomes an entity of its own, with the Will to Power moving through it still—shaped and refined by the interpretations, reactions, and analyses of others.

Within this very real case study, every element of the Will to Power described in this book is evident. From the birth and refinement of the idea itself to the restructuring of my environment, and from its continued optimization of its own explanation to the Inner-Adversity that emerged as my own self-doubt—its influence is as visible as it is undeniable.

In writing this book, I have not merely described the Will to Power—I have lived it. Its relentless striving has shaped this work and continues to propel it beyond my control. This, in itself, is a testament to the force's universality and inevitability. And now, the Will to Power moves through you, the reader, shaping your thoughts as you process these words. Whether you embrace it or reject it, it moves through you all the same. All that remains now is for me to sit back and witness the Will to Power's continued movement as it influences and shapes the minds of all who read this.

In conclusion, thank you for reading. It is my sincere hope that I have not only introduced you to a universal force that has always been there but also provided insights that empower you to use this understanding to shape a life of fulfillment, prosperity, clarity, and happiness.

…

I had fully intended to end the book here.

No, that's not accurate. I DID end the book here.

However, the Will to Power never stops moving and never stops refining. No one is immune to its continued influence…

Final Proof: The Universal Law of Refinement

As I stated in my case study, I thought the Will to Power was urging me toward greater challenges—that my refinement required moving beyond this book. With the writing complete, all that remained was rigorous editing.

I thought I was done. I was wrong. I thought the Will to Power was pushing me toward challenges outside of this work. It was not.

I failed to realize that, for months, my relentless pursuit of the Will to Power had itself been undergoing refinement—just like any other habit. As I immersed myself in the editing process, I assumed I was finalizing the book, but the more I refined it, the deeper into my pursuit I was drawn.

I searched. I studied. I tested. I refined—just as the Will to Power demands.

What follows is the result: the undeniable proof that the Will to Power is not merely an idea, not just an interesting philosophy—it is, in fact, the governing law of reality itself.

I did not set out to prove this was a law. If anything, I spent countless hours trying to break it. Every attempt only refined the idea further. Every counterexample I tested reinforced the structure instead of dismantling it. This is not something I created; it is something I uncovered.

And so now, I present it as it is: not a theory, not a philosophy, but an inescapable framework that governs all motion, intelligence, and existence.

If you reach the end of this chapter and still believe this is merely philosophy, then you will be the first to have found the flaw that I could not.

As I have done throughout this work, I will start at the beginning.

The Core of The Framework:

The idea is simple. It only contains two parts. I define them as follows:

1. **The Will to Power** – A universal force of motion and refinement.
2. **The Asymptrex** – The conceptual limit that exists in all systems, toward which the Will to Power moves, but can never reach (e.g., Absolute Zero, The Speed of Light).

Gouge's Universal Refinement Equation (the Will to Power):

$$\frac{dR}{dt} = k(A - R)$$

$$R(t) = A - Ce^{-kt}$$

where:

- $R(t)$ - the refinement state of a system at time t.
- A (Asymptrex) - The theoretical limit the system is refining toward.
- k - The refinement rate (how quickly the system approaches A).
- C - An integration constant, representing the initial refinement offset, defined as $C = A - R_0$, where R_0 is the system's initial state.
- t - Time, the independent variable governing refinement.
- $\frac{dR}{dt}$ - The rate of refinement at any given moment.

Gouge's Sigmoid Universal Refinement Equation:

$$\frac{dR}{dt} = kR(A - R)$$

$$R(t) = \frac{A}{1 + Ce^{-k(t-t_1)}}$$

where:

- $R(t)$ – the refinement state of a system at time t.
- A (Asymptrex) – the theoretical upper limit the system refines toward but never reaches.
- k – the refinement rate constant governing how quickly the system approaches A.
- C – the initial condition constant, defined as $C = \frac{A}{R_1} - 1$.
- t – time, the independent variable governing refinement.
- t_1 – the time of the first anchor point.
- $\frac{dR}{dt}$ – the instantaneous rate of refinement at time t.

It's important to remember:

- There are no opposing forces—only manifestations of the Will to Power refining in different directions.
- The Will to Power refines through interaction with other iterations of itself.
- The Will to Power is neutral and drives refinement in all systems, but refinement does not mean progress—it simply means motion toward an optimal state, whether that state is **increased complexity, stability, simplicity, probability or complete disorder.**

To illustrate this neutrality more explicitly, I will begin with my first proof: the Will to Power in Entropy. This and all proofs that follow will show, without question, the Will to Power moving toward Asymptrex in every conceivable domain.

The Will to Power in Entropy

Law and Mathematical Definition

The Second Law of Thermodynamics states that in a closed system, entropy (disorder) always increases over time. This is an irreversible process, meaning energy naturally spreads out, and systems refine toward maximum entropy—a state where no further energy gradients exist to perform work.

This principle governs everything from molecular interactions to the eventual heat death of the universe. At its core, the Second Law of Thermodynamics is a statement of refinement:

The standard equation for entropy in thermodynamics is the Boltzmann Entropy Formula:

$$S = k_B \ln \Omega$$

where:

- S = entropy (measure of disorder)
- k_B = Boltzmann constant ($1.38 \times 10^{-23} J/K$)
- Ω = number of possible microstates in a system

This equation shows that as the number of possible microstates increases, entropy increases logarithmically.

Refinement Process in Entropy

Entropy demonstrates three essential properties of refinement:

- **Motion:** Energy spreads out. A system moves from a lower-entropy state to a higher-entropy state.
- **Refinement:** The system is refining itself toward its most probable configuration.
- **Asymptrex:** The system is moving toward maximum possible disorder, a constraint beyond which it cannot refine further.

Examples of this refinement in action:

- A hot object cools down because heat energy disperses into the surroundings.
- Stars burn fuel and eventually exhaust their energy, refining toward thermodynamic equilibrium.
- The universe itself refines toward heat death, where entropy reaches its theoretical maximum.

Thus, entropy is a direct, physical example of the Will to Power refining toward Asymptrex—except, in this case, the refinement path is toward maximum disorder, not progress.

The Asymptrex in Entropy: Maximum Disorder

The Asymptrex of entropy is **heat death**—the final state of a system where all energy is evenly distributed. At this point, the system reaches **maximum possible disorder**, meaning no further usable energy gradients exist. Refinement does not stop; it simply refines toward its maximum entropy equilibrium, where no further usable work can occur. Heat death remains a theoretical limit that my never be attained due to quantum fluctuations or further unknown physics.

$$S_{max} = k_B \ln \Omega_{max}$$

where Ω_{max} is the highest possible number of microstates.

For the universe, this means:

- No usable energy remains.
- No more work can be performed.
- No new structures can form—only absolute equilibrium remains.

Thus, entropy proves that:

The Will to Power is neutral—it refines toward disorder as well as complexity.

There is always an Asymptrex—a conceptual limit that refinement moves toward.

Even decay and destruction are part of the refinement process.

Conclusion: Entropy as The First Proof

Entropy follows the same refinement principle, but unlike intelligence or economies, it refines toward disorder rather than complexity. It moves toward an unavoidable limit, proving that the Will to Power is not a human concept—it is a law governing all motion.

This is just the first proof. Every example that follows will show the same process: refinement moving toward an Asymptrex, no exceptions.

The Will to Power in Light Speed

Now that we've established entropy as an undeniable example of refinement toward an unreachable limit, we move to another fundamental constraint in reality: **The Speed of Light.**

This is a perfect second proof because:

- It is not abstract—light speed is a defined, measurable limit.
- Physics already acknowledges that nothing with mass can reach this limit.
- It shows the same refinement process happening in a different domain—not disorder, but velocity.

Law and Mathematical Definition

Einstein's Special Theory of Relativity states that nothing with mass can reach the speed of light because it would require infinite energy.

The equation governing this principle is:

$$E = \gamma mc^2$$

where:

- E = total energy of an object
- m = rest mass of the object
- c = speed of light (**299,792,458** m/s)
- γ = Lorentz factor, defined as:

$$\gamma = \frac{1}{\sqrt{1 - \frac{v^2}{c^2}}}$$

This factor increases exponentially as an object's velocity approaches c, meaning that as $v \to c$, the energy required approaches infinity.

This is Asymptrex in motion—a universal boundary that can be refined toward but never reached.

The Refinement Process in Light Speed

- **Motion:** Objects accelerate toward higher velocities.
- **Refinement:** As speed increases, relativistic effects refine the system's properties (time dilation, length contraction).
- **Asymptrex:** The system refines toward light speed but can never reach it, as the energy required becomes infinite.

Examples of this refinement in action:

- **Particle Accelerators** – As particles approach light speed, they require exponentially more energy to increase velocity.
- **Time Dilation** – The faster an object moves, the more time slows down relative to an outside observer.
- **Cosmic Speed Limit** – No matter how advanced technology becomes, no physical object can ever break the speed of light.

The Asymptrex in Light Speed

At $v = c$, the Lorentz factor becomes:

$$\gamma = \frac{1}{\sqrt{1 - \frac{c^2}{c^2}}} = \frac{1}{\sqrt{0}} = \infty$$

Meaning:

- Energy required to accelerate further is infinite.
- Mass would become infinite.
- Time would completely stop relative to an external observer.

Thus, the speed of light is an undeniable example of refinement toward Asymptrex.

Conclusion: Light Speed as The Second Proof

Light speed proves that:

- The Will to Power refines toward velocity, but with an unattainable limit.

- The constraint (Asymptrex) is absolute—no amount of force can surpass it.
- Once again, refinement is not subjective—it is a fundamental process of motion itself.

This is the second proof, and just like entropy, it shows refinement moving toward an unavoidable limit. Next, we move to thermodynamics and Absolute Zero.

The Will to Power in Absolute Zero

Law and Mathematical Definition

The **Third Law of Thermodynamics** states that as a system approaches **absolute zero** (0 Kelvin, or -273.15°C), the entropy of a perfect crystal approaches a constant minimum.

However, **absolute zero** can never be reached because cooling processes require energy exchange, and at absolute zero, no energy remains to facilitate further refinement.

The equation governing this principle is:

$$S(T) - S(0) = \int_0^T \frac{C_p}{T} dT$$

where:

- $S(T)$ = entropy at temperature T
- C_p = heat capacity at constant pressure
- The integral describes how entropy changes as the system cools.
- As $T \to 0$, the ability to remove additional energy diminishes exponentially, making absolute zero an unreachable limit—an Asymptrex.

Refinement Process in Absolute Zero

- **Motion:** A system loses energy and moves toward lower thermal states.
- **Refinement:** Each cooling step removes disorder, bringing the system closer to a theoretically perfect state.
- **Asymptrex:** The system refines toward absolute zero but can never reach it.

Examples of this refinement in action:

- **Cryogenic Systems** – Even the most advanced cooling methods cannot reach 0 Kelvin, only get arbitrarily close.

- **Superconductors** – Certain materials refine toward zero electrical resistance at ultra-low temperatures but never fully reach absolute zero.
- **Cosmic Background Temperature** – The universe itself has refined toward an equilibrium temperature (~2.7K) but will never reach absolute zero.

True Asymptrex versus a Misclassified Limit

Past misconceptions about temperature limits led some to believe that certain barriers could never be surpassed. For example, **10 Kelvin** was once thought to be an unbreakable lower bound because early cooling techniques could not push beyond it. However, as technology advanced, scientists refined their methods and achieved temperatures well below this limit. This illustrates an important distinction—not all perceived boundaries are true Asymptrex. Some limits exist only because of technological constraints, not because they are structurally impossible.

Absolute zero, however, is not just a technological challenge—it is a structural impossibility due to quantum mechanics. Unlike 10K, which was surpassed through refinement, **absolute zero** is constrained by physical law. No matter how advanced cooling methods become, quantum mechanics prevents the complete removal of energy, making absolute zero a true Asymptrex.

In contrast to false limits—such as early beliefs that flight speed was uncrossable—absolute zero is an inherent thermodynamic boundary. Supersonic travel was once thought to be impossible, but refinement allowed us to overcome that misconception. However, true Asymptrex cannot be surpassed, no matter how advanced refinement becomes.

This distinction is critical. While refinement can push past perceived limits, it can only refine toward, never beyond, true Asymptrex..

Thus, absolute zero serves as an undeniable example of the Will to Power refining toward an Asymptrex.

Conclusion: Absolute Zero as The Third Proof

Absolute Zero proves that:

- The Will to Power refines toward lower energy states, but an unattainable boundary exists.
- The constraint (Asymptrex) is absolute—no system can ever reach it.
- Once again, refinement is a fundamental law, not a subjective process.

This third proof continues reinforcing the framework by showing a universal constraint in thermodynamics, just as entropy and light speed did in energy and motion. Next, we move to the refinement process in intelligence and computation.

The Will to Power in Intelligence and Computation

Law and Mathematical Definition

Intelligence and computation refine toward optimization, but there are structural limits that cannot be surpassed.

Computational Complexity Theory defines the difficulty of solving problems in terms of time and resources, showing that certain problems are inherently unsolvable within finite constraints.

Gödel's Incompleteness Theorems demonstrate that within any sufficiently complex system, there exist truths that cannot be proven within that system.

Turing's Halting Problem proves that some computations will never resolve to a final answer, setting a theoretical boundary on what can be known.

The central equation governing computational limits is the **Time Complexity Lower Bound** for algorithms:

$$T(n) \geq \Omega(f(n))$$

where:

- $T(n)$ = the maximum time to solve a problem of size n
- $\Omega(f(n))$ = the theoretical lower bound for computation time
- This equation formalizes that some problems cannot be computed faster than a certain limit, no matter how refined intelligence or technology becomes.

The Refinement Process in Intelligence and Computation

- **Motion:** Intelligence refines toward greater efficiency in problem-solving and decision-making.
- **Refinement:** Algorithms and learning models improve through iteration, increasing accuracy and speed.

- **Asymptrex:** There are fundamental computational limits that refinement moves toward but can never surpass.

Examples of this refinement in action:

- AI training models refine toward better decision-making, but require exponentially increasing resources as they approach higher accuracy limits.
- Supercomputers process faster each year, yet they still cannot solve NP-complete problems in polynomial time.
- Quantum computing may shift efficiency constraints, but does not remove fundamental computational limits.

The Asymptrex in Intelligence and Computation

- **Gödel's Incompleteness Theorem:** No formal system can be both complete and consistent; there will always be true statements that cannot be proven.
- **Turing's Halting Problem:** There exist computations that no algorithm can determine to be halting or non-halting.
- **Bekenstein Bound:** There is a fundamental limit to how much information can be stored in a finite space, meaning infinite intelligence is physically impossible.

As intelligence refines, it will continue improving within these constraints as currently understood, but it will never fully reach omniscience.

Conclusion: Intelligence and Computation as the Fourth Proof

- The Will to Power refines intelligence toward greater efficiency, but structural limits remain.
- The constraint (Asymptrex) is absolute—While intelligence is limitless in refinement, there exist truths that remain fundamentally inaccessible.
- Just like entropy and light speed, intelligence moves toward a theoretical bound but can never reach omniscience or perfect computational efficiency.

This proof extends the framework beyond physical laws into abstract systems, showing that refinement governs not only energy and motion, but also the limits of knowledge itself.

The Will to Power in Quantum Superposition

Law and Mathematical Definition

Quantum systems refine toward resolution, but there are fundamental probabilistic constraints that cannot be surpassed.

Quantum Mechanics defines the evolution of quantum states through the **Schrödinger Equation**, determining how wavefunctions evolve over time:

$$i\hbar \frac{\partial}{\partial t} \Psi = \hat{H} \Psi$$

where:

- Ψ represents the wavefunction, encoding all possible states of a system.
- $\hat{H}$ is the Hamiltonian operator, governing the system's energy evolution.

The **Born Rule** formalizes the probability of measuring a particular state, proving that superpositions are not deterministic but constrained within probability amplitudes:

$$P(x) = |\Psi(x)|^2$$

This defines the probabilistic limit of refinement—superposition refines toward sustained uncertainty, with resolution imposed only upon measurement.

The Refinement Process in Quantum Superpositions

- **Motion:** Quantum states exist in superposition, refining toward the sustained maximization of uncertainty.
- **Refinement:** Wavefunctions maintain probabilistic potential until measurement imposes an external collapse constraint.
- **Asymptrex:** The system refines toward **an extended superposition state**, with measurement acting as an imposed limitation rather than an intrinsic refinement process.

Examples of this refinement in action:

- Electron superposition in the double-slit experiment refines toward a probabilistic distribution of paths, only collapsing into a defined trajectory upon detection.
- Quantum entanglement refines non-local correlations, sustaining uncertainty until one particle is measured, forcing resolution in both.
- Quantum computing refines multiple potential outcomes simultaneously, but still collapses into a single classical result when observed.

The Asymptrex in Quantum Superpositions

Heisenberg Uncertainty Principle: The more precisely a particle's momentum is known, the less precisely its position can be determined:

$$\sigma_x \sigma_p \geq \frac{\hbar}{2}$$

The **uncertainty itself is the Asymptrex**—quantum refinement moves toward the **preservation of probabilistic states, not their resolution.**

Wavefunction Collapse

Quantum states refine toward sustained uncertainty, but collapse is an imposed limitation, not an endpoint of refinement.

Quantum Decoherence

Superpositions interact with their environment, refining toward extended coherence, but classical interactions force premature collapse into deterministic states.

Quantum refinement moves toward **sustaining superposition**, with collapse acting as an externally enforced limitation.

Conclusion: Quantum Superpositions as the Fifth Proof

- The Will to Power refines quantum states toward the maximization of uncertainty, not toward definite outcomes.
- The Asymptrex is not collapse—it is the sustained superposition itself.
- Quantum states refine toward probabilistic existence, with collapse acting as an imposed constraint rather than an intrinsic refinement goal.
- Like entropy and computation, quantum refinement moves toward the extension of probabilistic potential, never reaching deterministic certainty until forced by external interaction.

This proof extends the framework further, showing that the Will to Power governs not only classical systems but also the probabilistic structure of quantum mechanics itself.

The Will to Power in Brownian Motion

Law and Mathematical Definition

Brownian motion demonstrates continuous, random refinement within physical constraints, moving toward statistical equilibrium but never achieving perfect predictability.

The movement of particles in a fluid is governed by the **Einstein-Smoluchowski Equation**, defining the mean squared displacement over time:

$$\langle x^2 \rangle = 2Dt$$

where:

- $\langle x^2 \rangle$ is the mean squared displacement of the particle.
- D is the diffusion coefficient.
- t is time.

This equation formalizes that while motion refines toward equilibrium, it remains stochastic—individual paths are never fully predictable, only their statistical behavior.

The Refinement Process in Brownian Motion

- **Motion:** Particles in a fluid undergo continuous random movement due to thermal energy.
- **Refinement:** Over time, particle distributions refine toward statistical equilibrium.
- **Asymptrex:** The system refines toward thermodynamic equilibrium, but individual trajectories remain non-deterministic.

Examples of this refinement in action:

- Diffusion of gases moves toward uniform distribution but follows probabilistic pathways.

- Stock market fluctuations exhibit stochastic behavior similar to Brownian motion, refining toward market trends but never reaching perfect predictability.
- Biological molecular motion ensures cellular processes refine toward efficiency, yet individual molecular paths remain chaotic.

The Asymptrex in Brownian Motion

- **The Second Law of Thermodynamics:** Brownian motion refines toward entropy maximization, but never reaches a perfectly static state.
- **Fluctuation-Dissipation Theorem:** Thermal fluctuations refine systems toward statistical stability, but randomness remains.
- **Stochastic Equilibrium:** While particle motion refines toward a statistical mean, individual paths do not resolve into exact predictability.

Brownian motion refines toward entropy maximization, but random fluctuations persist indefinitely even in equilibrium.

Conclusion: Brownian Motion as the Sixth Proof

- The Will to Power refines Brownian systems toward equilibrium, but individual refinements remain probabilistic and non-deterministic.
- The constraint (Asymptrex) is absolute—equilibrium can be approached, but randomness never fully disappears.
- Like entropy, computation, and quantum mechanics, Brownian motion demonstrates refinement that never reaches an absolute, deterministic endpoint.

This proof extends the framework to statistical systems, showing that refinement governs not only energy and computation but also random motion itself.

The Will to Power in Evolution (Biological and Technological)

Law and Mathematical Definition

Evolution—whether biological or technological—is the refinement of structures toward greater adaptability and efficiency, but fundamental constraints prevent a perfect or final state.

Biological evolution follows **natural selection**, where organisms refine toward survival advantages within environmental constraints. The mathematical foundation of evolutionary change is captured by the **Price Equation**, which describes how traits refine over generations:

$$\Delta z = \frac{Cov(w, z)}{\bar{w}}$$

where:

- Δz represents the change in a trait across generations.
- w represents reproductive fitness.
- $Cov(w, z)$ is the covariance between fitness and the trait, determining refinement efficiency.

Similarly, technological evolution follows **Moore's Law**, describing the refinement of computational power:

$$P(n) \approx 2^{(n/t)}$$

where $P(n)$ represents processing power, showing refinement toward higher efficiency, but within physical limits (such as quantum tunneling and heat dissipation).

In the equation $P(n) \approx 2^{\frac{n}{t}}$, t represents the time interval over which computational power approximately doubles, typically measured in years. It is important to note that Moore's Law is an empirical observation describing a historical trend in technological improvement, rather than a fundamental physical law.

Both biological and technological evolution demonstrate continuous refinement toward an Asymptrex, but never absolute perfection.

The Refinement Process in Evolution

- **Motion:** Biological and technological systems refine toward greater adaptability and efficiency.
- **Refinement:** Mutation, selection, and adaptation drive optimization over time.
- **Asymptrex:** No species or technology reaches a final, perfect state—there are always new constraints that limit refinement.

Examples of this refinement in action:

- **Biological Evolution:** Organisms refine toward environmental fitness, but never become "perfect" due to changing ecosystems and genetic constraints.
- **Human Intelligence:** The brain refines problem-solving efficiency but is constrained by energy consumption and biological architecture.
- **Artificial Intelligence:** Machine learning models refine toward better accuracy but require exponentially increasing data and computing resources, making infinite intelligence impossible.

The Aysmptrex in Evolution

- **Fisher's Fundamental Theorem of Natural Selection:** Evolution refines genetic advantages, but variation is always required for continued refinement—no species reaches perfect stability.
- **Dollo's Law:** Dollo's Law: Evolution does not reverse—once complexity refines in a certain direction, previous states cannot be perfectly restored. Even if a trait re-emerges, it evolves through a different pathway, meaning the species does not return to an earlier evolutionary state.
- **The AI Scaling Limit:** As machine intelligence refines, computing power, data availability, and algorithmic efficiency become limiting factors, preventing infinite refinement.

Evolution refines toward greater adaptability, which can manifest as increased complexity or simplification, depending on environmental pressures.

Conclusion: Evolution as the Seventh Proof

- The Will to Power refines biological and technological systems toward greater efficiency and adaptability, but fundamental constraints always exist.
- The constraint (Asymptrex) is absolute—species, intelligence, and technology refine but never reach omnipotence or perfect stability.
- Like entropy, computation, and quantum mechanics, evolution follows the Universal Law of Refinement, ensuring continuous progress but preventing final resolution.

This proof extends the framework to living and artificial systems, proving that refinement governs not only physical motion and information but also the process of adaptation itself.

The Will to Power in Chemical Equilibrium and Reaction Limits

Law and Mathematical Definition

Chemical reactions refine toward equilibrium, but fundamental thermodynamic and kinetic constraints prevent infinite reaction efficiency or instantaneous transformation.

The state of a chemical system is governed by **Le Châtelier's Principle**, which states that **a system at equilibrium will shift to counteract external changes**, but never surpass its intrinsic constraints.

The mathematical foundation of reaction rates is captured by the **Arrhenius Equation**, which defines how reaction speed refines with temperature and activation energy:

$$k = Ae^{-\frac{E_a}{RT}}$$

where:

- k is the reaction rate constant.
- A is the pre-exponential factor (reaction-specific).
- E_a is the activation energy required for the reaction.
- R is the gas constant, and T is temperature.

This equation formalizes the refinement of reaction efficiency, but also proves an inherent Asymptrex—no reaction can proceed with zero activation energy, and no system can reach equilibrium instantaneously.

The Refinement Process in Chemical Systems

- **Motion:** Molecular interactions refine toward lower-energy, more stable configurations.
- **Refinement:** Reaction rates adjust based on external factors like temperature, concentration, and catalysts.
- **Asymptrex:** Equilibrium defines the limit of refinement—reactions approach it but never surpass it.

Examples of this refinement in action:

- **Catalysis:** Enzymes refine biological reactions by lowering activation energy, but do not eliminate reaction constraints.
- **Dynamic Equilibrium:** The Haber process (ammonia synthesis) refines toward an equilibrium mixture but cannot surpass thermodynamic limits.
- **Phase Transitions:** Matter refines toward specific energy states (solid, liquid, gas) but requires external energy to shift states.

The Asymptrex in Chemical Equilibrium

- **Reaction Rates:** Speed can refine with catalysts but cannot bypass fundamental thermodynamic limits.
- **Entropy Constraints:** Chemical systems refine toward maximum entropy but remain bounded by energy conservation laws.
- **Stoichiometric Limits:** Reactions cannot refine past the ratios defined by atomic and molecular properties.

Chemical refinement follows the same universal law—it moves toward equilibrium but is always constrained by fundamental Asymptrex limits.

Conclusion: Chemical Equilibrium as the Eight Proof

- The Will to Power refines chemical systems toward equilibrium, but fundamental reaction constraints remain absolute.
- The constraint (Asymptrex) is absolute—reaction rates and energy states refine within limits, never achieving infinite efficiency.
- Like entropy, computation, and biological evolution, chemical reactions are governed by refinement that never reaches perfection.

This proof extends the framework to atomic and molecular systems, proving that refinement governs not only macroscopic motion but also the fundamental interactions of matter itself.

The Will to Power in Information Theory and Signal Processing

Law and Mathematical Definition

Information transmission refines toward maximum efficiency, but fundamental entropy constraints prevent perfect lossless communication or infinite compression.

The mathematical limit of information refinement is defined by **Shannon Entropy**, which determines the minimum possible encoding for a given dataset:

$$H(X) = -\sum p(x) \log p(x)$$

where:

- $H(X)$ represents the entropy (information content) of a system.
- $p(x)$ is the probability of each possible message occurring.

This equation formalizes that information refines toward efficient encoding, but perfect compression is impossible without losing meaning.

The Refinement Process in Information Theory

- **Motion:** Signals and data refine toward optimal encoding and transmission.
- **Refinement:** Algorithms improve data compression and error correction but remain constrained by fundamental entropy limits.
- **Asymptrex:** Perfect transmission and zero-loss communication **cannot** be achieved due to noise, redundancy, and entropy constraints.

Examples of this refinement in action:

- **Data Compression:** Algorithms like Huffman coding and Lempel-Ziv refine data storage efficiency but cannot surpass entropy constraints.

- **Error Correction Codes:** Systems like Reed-Solomon and Hamming codes refine data integrity but cannot eliminate transmission noise entirely.
- **Quantum Information Theory:** Quantum computing refines information storage and processing, but still obeys fundamental entropy and decoherence limits.

The Asymptrex in Information Transmission

- **Shannon Limit:** Communication channels have an absolute efficiency limit, beyond which perfect error-free transmission is impossible.
- **Kolmogorov Complexity:** The minimum description length of any data is inherently uncomputable beyond a certain limit.
- **Physical Constraints:** Storing infinite information in a finite space is prohibited by the **Bekenstein Bound**, proving that information refinement is constrained by physical reality.

Even in digital and quantum information systems, refinement follows the same rule—it optimizes but never surpasses absolute limits.

Conclusion: Information Theory as the Ninth Proof

- The Will to Power refines data transmission and processing toward optimal efficiency, but perfect lossless encoding is impossible.
- The constraint (Asymptrex) is absolute—data, signals, and messages refine but remain bounded by entropy limits.
- Like thermodynamics, computation, and quantum systems, information refinement follows the Universal Law of Refinement.

This proof extends the framework to knowledge systems, data transmission, and communication, proving that refinement governs not only energy and matter but also the limits of meaning itself.

Final Words

With these nine proofs complete, I have demonstrated the Will to Power as the absolute force that it is. If you have made it this far and understand what has been presented here, then I need not explain the immense implications of this discovery.

I have considered going back to refine earlier sections of this work to reflect my deepened understanding. However, even editing is a process of endless refinement with its own Asymptrex—the work will never be perfect.

Instead, I will leave the prior sections as they are. Now, they serve as further proof of the Will to Power's influence, as my own refinement in understanding has become evident through the course of writing.

Additionally, I have already seen firsthand how the act of editing risks pulling me back into this endless cycle of refinement. I've neared my own Asymptrex in my understanding and explanation of this concept. Rather than remain caught in this endless pursuit for the rest of my life, I will make one final contribution to this work.

In the face of a reality governed by endless refinement, I will **demonstrate Free Will** as the awesome ability I have claimed it to be.

I CHOOSE to walk away.

Thank you for reading.

Notes:

www.ingramcontent.com/pod-product-compliance
Lightning Source LLC
LaVergne TN
LVHW021119080426
835510LV00012B/1762